Early Chinese Metalwork

in the Collection of the Seattle Art Museum

Michael Knight

Early Chinese Metalwork is the seventh in a series of guides highlighting the Seattle Art Museum collections. Other titles include:
Egyptian Art
Ivories
African Art from Crocodiles to Convertibles
East African Art
Katagami: Japanese Textile Stencils
Classical Vases and Containers

This publication has been generously supported by a grant from the National Endowment for the Arts. Additional support has been provided by SAMS (Seattle Art Museum Supporters).

Printed in Japan
ISBN 0-932216-31-5
LC 89-060450

Designed by Corinna Campbell
Photography by Paul Macapia
Illustrations by Sharon Birzer

cover: Shang dynasty *jue* dating from the mid second millennium through the late 12th to 11th century B.C.

Foreword

The Seattle Art Museum's holdings of early Chinese bronzes offer an overview of this remarkable area of artistic accomplishment. This publication, the seventh in an ongoing series, details the museum's metalwork from the early Bronze Age to the Western Han dynasty. Although Chinese bronzes were not a primary interest of the museum's cofounder and long-time director, Dr. Richard E. Fuller, an impressive group of bronzes has been assembled mostly during the 1940s and 1950s. Two notable additions have been acquired in recent years. This publication emphasizes the collection's strength in ceremonial vessels; the Seattle Art Museum collection also includes bronze objects for personal adornment.

This book surveys a topic of particular interest to its author, Michael Knight, associate curator of Asian art. Though precise analysis of the function of these vessels still eludes scholars, the technical and stylistic development and cryptic surface decorations of these bronze vessels have, as demonstrated in Knight's concise text, been carefully studied. Knight makes apparent an animate parade of beasts that cover a delicate Shang dynasty handle and how with the *taotie* Chinese artisans gave flat form three-dimensional life. He decodes decorative patterns and deftly articulates, if not why, how and when these wares were made.

Patterson Sims
Associate Director for Art
and Exhibitions

Chinese Metalwork from the Early Bronze Age to the Western Han Dynasty

The study of the Bronze Age arts of China (early second millennium B.C. – c. 500 B.C.) has progressed tremendously in recent decades. Newly discovered sites and the re-investigation of artifacts, in the light of these discoveries, has made it possible to discuss with some confidence the technical issues faced during the Bronze Age by Chinese artisans working in metal. This monograph explores some of these issues in relation to a choice group of ritual bronzes dating from the Shang to the Western Han dynasties (mid second millennium B.C. – A.D. 9) in the collection of the Seattle Art Museum. The discussion is dictated somewhat by the makeup of the collection. For example the Western Zhou dynasty is represented only by the *gui* (no. 9) and the *you* (no. 10) which provide some evidence of trends at the beginning of the period, but do not allow for an in-depth analysis of important issues such as regionalism, changes in ritual practice, or stylistic developments. Discussion of foreign influence, a factor of particular significance in the late Spring and Autumn and Warring States periods (late seventh – third century B.C.), is limited because the collection has no examples that directly demonstate it. This monograph focuses largely on technical issues; although iconography and useage are referred to, a full discussion would require a depth of social, economic, religious, and philosophical study beyond the scope of this publication.

This discussion is divided into three sections. The first explores the development of Shang dynasty (mid second millennium – mid eleventh century B.C.) ritual bronzes from ceramic prototypes of the Neolithic period (fourth millennium B.C.– early second millennium B.C.), an increased awareness and exploitation of the new medium of bronze, and the evolution of a vocabulary of decorative motifs. The second section deals with the bronzes of the Western Zhou dynasty and Spring and Autumn period (mid eleventh century – c. 480 B.C.) when the technology of bronze casting had developed sufficiently to be adapted to changes in decoration and function induced by changes in ritual and philosophy, as well as by a developing sense of regionalism. The third section covers the Warring States period to the early Western Han dynasty (c. 480 – second century B.C.). During this period, other materials competed successfully with bronze, and a final flurry of innovation occurred as the bronze industry attempted to meet this competition.

I: The Early Bronze Age

Bronze presented both exciting new possibilities and challenges to the Chinese as they emerged from the Neolithic period. Because of its unique characteristics, it offered a greater range of function and decoration than did clay, stone, wood, and the other media available at the time. For weapons, tools, and utensils bronze provided an expanded range of shapes, a keener and more uniform edge, and greater strength. Once the technology for casting bronze was developed, large numbers of such implements could be created with a lower investment of time and energy than preparing the less durable ones they replaced.

The greatest initial challenges to exploiting this new medium were finding reliable sources for the necessary ores and fuels, developing appropriate formulas for bronze alloys, creating foundries that performed consistently, and developing an appropriate system for casting. By the early second millennium B.C. ritual bronzes began to appear in numbers and basic solutions to these challenges had been found, although experimentation and new discoveries continued throughout the Bronze Age.

While technologies developed for the multiple casting of weapons, tools, and utensils, the majority of bronze ritual vessels of Bronze Age China were created in a complicated clay piece-mold technique that allowed only a single vessel from each cast. The first step involved making a model of the vessel in clay; some or all of the decoration was created on the surface of this model. Next, slabs of damp clay were applied to the model to take an impression of its shape and decoration; these slabs were then removed to be used as the mold. The original model became the core for the mold by shaving enough material from its surface to equal the desired thickness of walls of the vessel. In many examples additional carving or other refinement of the decoration was done on the surface of the mold before it was assembled over the core.[1] The entire ensemble was almost certainly heated before casting to prevent the shock of contact with the molten metal from shattering the mold and to allow the metal to flow into all areas without solidifying too soon. Vents must have been positioned to allow the escape of the superheated gasses produced by this process.

The advantage of this technique was that the greatest part of the creative process was carried out in clay, a familiar material; the shapes and many of the decorative motifs found on the earliest bronze vessels were inherited from a vocabulary developed in Neolithic ceramics. However, these shapes and motifs were not always suited to the process of creating vessels of bronze, nor did they allow the full exploitation of its unique qualities. The evolution of the shapes and decoration of bronze vessels during the Shang dynasty reveals a progressive proficiency with the new medium and an increasing independence of bronze manufacture from its Neolithic wood, ceramic, or stone prototypes.

Because of the complexities of the shapes and the limitations of casting, the ceramic mold for the bronze vessel was multisectional. The mold had to be designed to allow ease of reassembly after separation from the model and to minimize the visual effects of the inevitable mold lines on the decoration of the finished vessel. Thus, motifs either had to continue through the mold sections, or they had to be designed to be divided in the same manner as the mold. Also, because the mold was taken from an existing model, it was impossible to create surfaces such as openwork or multiple layers with voids between them. Decoration on these vessels therefore was usually limited to the exterior surface except for inscriptions, which most frequently appeared on the interior.[2] Complicated three-dimensional elements such as handles and legs presented particular difficulties. In some examples these elements were precast, placed in the appropriate position in the main mold, and the object cast onto them. In other cases, the main shape or body of a vessel was cast first, the mold for the handle or leg was attached to it, and the appendage was then cast onto the vessel. Only in later periods was there extensive use of techniques such as soldering, lost-wax casting, or others.

Most surviving bronze vessels of the early Bronze Age in China were designed for serving food or wine in the rituals of the aristocracy. These rituals were carried out in a prescribed manner, with the number, type, and scale of the vessel determined by the occasion and the status of the participants. The majority of these rituals involved ancestor worship: sacrifice to ancestors was a method to attain their assistance in a variety of endeavors, ranging from appeasing deities, to assuring success at war, to predicting the appropriate time to plant crops.

The foods and wines presented in these sacrifices were served warm, and many ritual bronze vessels accommodate placement on a fire through legs or ring feet. Vessels were also displayed on large bronze altars, some of which served as stoves. These ritual vessels can be divided by use into two very broad types: those intended for serving food, and those for serving wine and other liquids. Ritual objects such as bells appeared as changes in technology allowed and ritual required.[3]

Function created definite challenges in vessel design and the arrangement of decoration, particularly for the types of wine vessels that were intended to pour. To facilitate pouring, such vessels are usually long in one axis and narrow in the other; for the same reason, curved surfaces are much more common than flat, and most types have a handle and spout. Food vessels, on the other hand, tend to be more balanced and symmetrical. Food was served with a ladle; therefore either flat or uniformly round surfaces were acceptable. Handles on food vessels were used only to move the vessel, and thus could be positioned so as not to interfere with the balance of the design or the decoration.

Certain motifs appear with great regularity as surface decoration on vessels of the early Bronze Age; unfortunately contemporary written materials do not reveal their meaning. Many designs consist of composite or wholly imaginary animals. On bronze vessels of the Shang dynasty, the most frequently seen of these animals is the *taotie,* a creature whose body has been "split" down the midline starting at the head and portrayed in mirror-image halves on the body of the vessel. The head has large eyes, horns, and a gaping mouth; the body, at times, has only one pair of legs.[4] In later periods of the Shang dynasty, the *taotie* was joined on these vessels by a wide range of dragons, birds, and other animals, both real and imaginary.

Changing responses to the technical and artistic challenges presented by bronze can be seen in the group of three *jue* (nos. 1-3). The *jue* is a wine vessel and one of only a very few types of ritual vessels that are asymmetrical. The *jue* was a shape inherited from a Neolithic ceramic prototype and is also the earliest surviving bronze vessel. The asymmetrical form and positioning of handle, spout, and legs were easily accomplished in ceramic but presented design and technical challenges in bronze, particularly in piece-mold casting. Each of the three vessels illustrated demonstrates a different approach to these challenges, with an overall evolution away from the ceramic prototype to a fuller exploitation of the unique characteristics of bronze.

In the earliest of these three *jue* (no. 1), which may be dated roughly to the mid second millennium B.C.,[5] the challenges of creating this asymmetrical form have been met by dividing the vessel into four sections: spout, upper body, lower body, and legs. The legs are connected to the flat bottom and are therefore visually separate from the rest of the vessel. This additive approach is inherited from ceramics. However, the thin casting of elements such as the lip, the blade-shaped legs, and the abrupt transition at the bottom of the vessel would not have been successful in ceramic and reveal a long experimentation with a variety of approaches to working with metal.

This *jue* was created in a three-section

Left to right: No. 1. *Jue,* Shang dynasty, mid second millenium B.C., 9 1/8″ x 6 3/4″, gift of Mr. and Mrs. Herbert Brink, 62.101; No. 2. *Jue,* Shang dynasty, mid–late second millennium B.C., 7 7/8″ x 7″, Eugene Fuller Memorial Collection, 34.63; No. 3. Jue, Shang dynasty, late Anyang period, late 12th–mid 11th century B.C., 9 5/16″ x 7 3/8″, Eugene Fuller Memorial Collection, 49.200

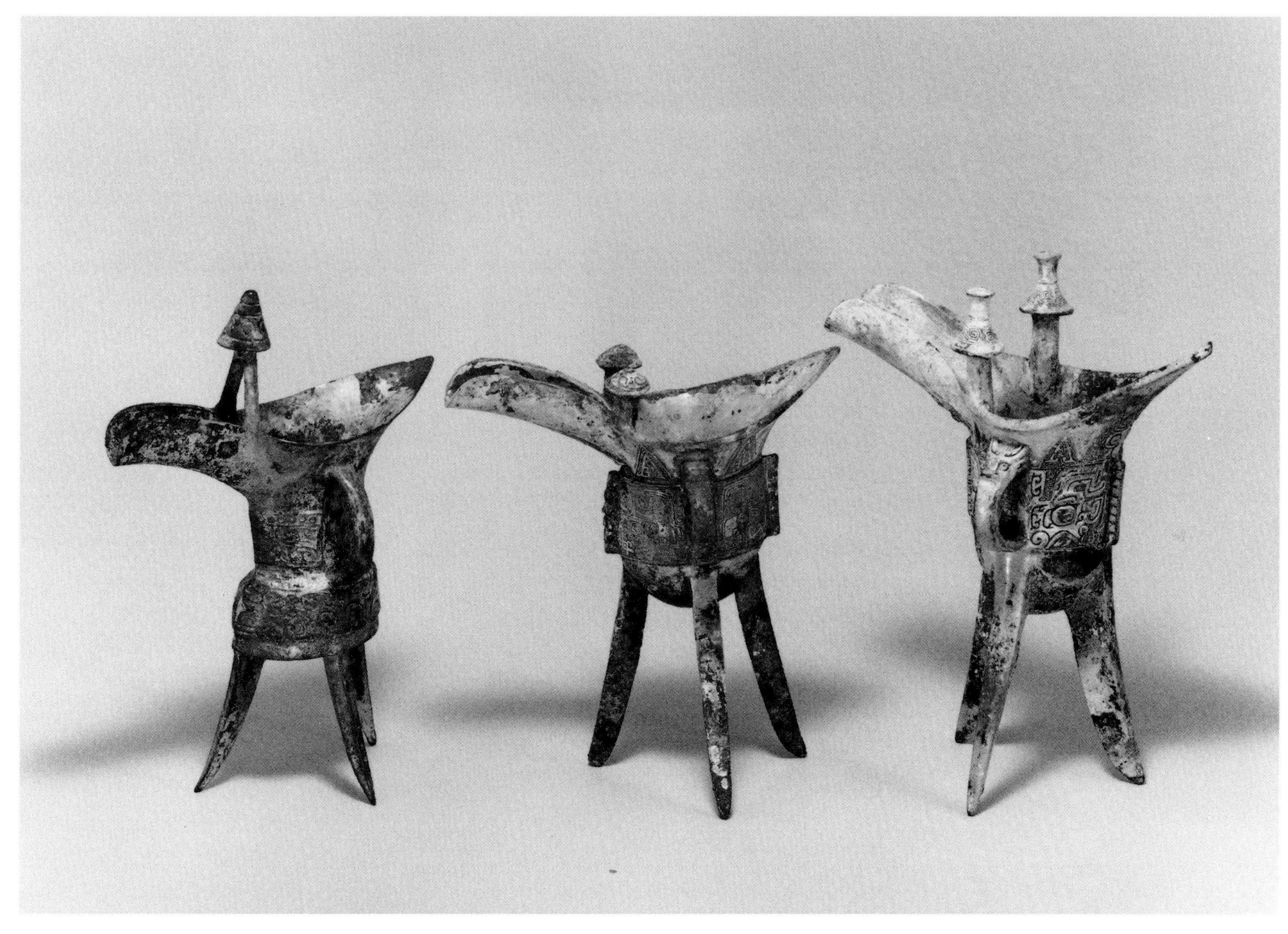

mold; the legs are positioned one at each mold line. This made it possible to create the vessel with its three legs and handle in one casting. However, the vessel is two-sided, with decoration symmetrically arranged on both sides; using a three-part mold, it was nearly impossible to prevent the mold lines from interfering with the decoration. This problem was increased by the placement of the handle in relation to the decoration, the legs, and the spout. The solution here was achieved by applying the designs in two horizontal bands. Only the upper band is influenced by the presence of the handle, where the main motif is separated and displayed on either side of it. However, one mold line goes through the center of the bottom mask and across the area covered by the handle. The decoration on the side opposite the handle is not affected by mold lines.

In this early *jue,* the decoration on the upper level is in thin thread relief, and the lower section is in broader elements. It is likely that the thread relief decoration was created in the mold, rather than on the model; the technical difficulty of carving away the entire field in order to leave a complex pattern of thin thread design in relief on a model is far greater than the relative simplicity of carving the design into the mold. The lower band of decoration, however, may have been carved on the model and refined on the mold.[6] This vessel exhibits a relatively early example of the *taotie.* This creature has large bulging eyes, a spade-shaped device on its forehead, inverted C-shaped horns, and a long, thin body; on the upper band it has a split tail.

Although prototypes of the motifs on this vessel can be found in Neolithic ceramics, the use of fine thread relief was a new development in bronze. Because of the strength and resiliency of the medium and the nature of the casting technique employed, such designs were easily accomplished on bronze ritual vessels. Thread relief, which was a translation of decoration incised in a ceramic mold, was a logical step in a trend toward adding raised surface designs on bronze vessels. The exploration of this potential was one of the major factors in the evolution of decorative styles during the early Bronze Age. This type of decoration was less suited to ceramics. To avoid breakage, the majority of surface designs on ceramics were painted or incised, or else were of larger scale and with rounded profiles. Fine thread relief could easily be created on ceramic through applications to the surface. However, because of their fragile nature, such designs damaged easily and would have rendered a ceramic vessel decorated in this fashion nearly unusable.

The second in this series of *jue* (no. 2), which can be dated to the mid to late second millennium B.C., presents a different point of departure for both design and decoration than the earlier example.[7] Unlike the earlier *jue,* with its four distinct sections, this piece is visually unified. The spout, body, and legs are integrated parts of an overall design. The area below the handle, which was flat-bottomed and carried a distinct band of decoration on the earlier *jue,* has been replaced by a rounded section without decoration that continues below the point of attachment for the legs. Although much simpler, this design is not entirely aesthetically successful; the body proportion is rather squat, and the symmetrical arrangement of the spout and the decoration has not been fully aligned with the asymmetrical arrangement of the three legs or the off-center position of the handle.

On this *jue,* three flanges and the handle serve to divide the surface decoration into four nearly equal sections. The space under the handle has been filled with a two-

Front view of the *jue* (no. 1).

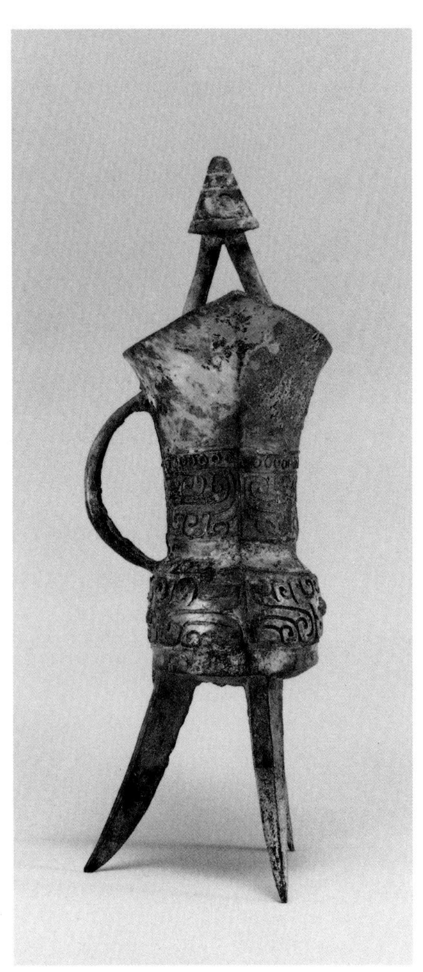

character inscription. The decor band is tied visually to the spout by seven blade-shaped devices, one on the underside of the spout, one at the back of the spout, three on the side opposite the handle, and one on either side of the handle; the handle takes the place of the third blade design. Thus, the decor serves to unify the body, the spout, and the handle of the vessel into a coherent unit, and the presence of the handle has been balanced by the addition of the flanges and the blade-shaped motifs.[8]

The balance achieved in the upper section of the vessel does not continue through the transition between the body and the legs. This owes in part to the difficulty of aligning the four-part decoration with the three legs and also to the limitations of the piece-mold technique. Although there are no visible mold lines, it is almost certain this vessel was created in a three-part mold, with the lines of division at the legs. This vessel was created in one cast. There is no evidence that the legs were cast separately and attached to the vessel or that the vessel was cast onto the legs. The result is that two of the flanges are located just out of alignment with two of the legs, and the handle is directly above the third; the entire vessel is thus heavily weighted toward the side with the handle.

The flanges that descend from the front and back of the spout divide the single band of decoration into two sections that are each divided in half again, one by a third flange, the other by the handle opposite it. Although flanges also appear on certain Neolithic ceramics, the sharp edges, fine detail, and small openings cut through those on this vessel would be impractical on a ceramic vessel. The development of elaborate flanges is an example of the bronze caster's further experimentation with three-dimensional designs on the surface.

As in the earlier *jue,* the main motif is the *taotie,* and one main mask appears on each side of the vessel. In this later *jue,* the broader main motifs are surrounded by a pattern of finer designs, early examples of spiral designs known as *leiwen.* However, the graphic distinction between the motifs is not entirely clear, resulting in some confusion between parts of the *taotie* mask and the *leiwen.* A small pendant dragon flanked by a horizontal motif is located in the lower corner of each of the four sections of the design next to the flanges. The differences

Three-quarter back view of the *jue* (no. 2).

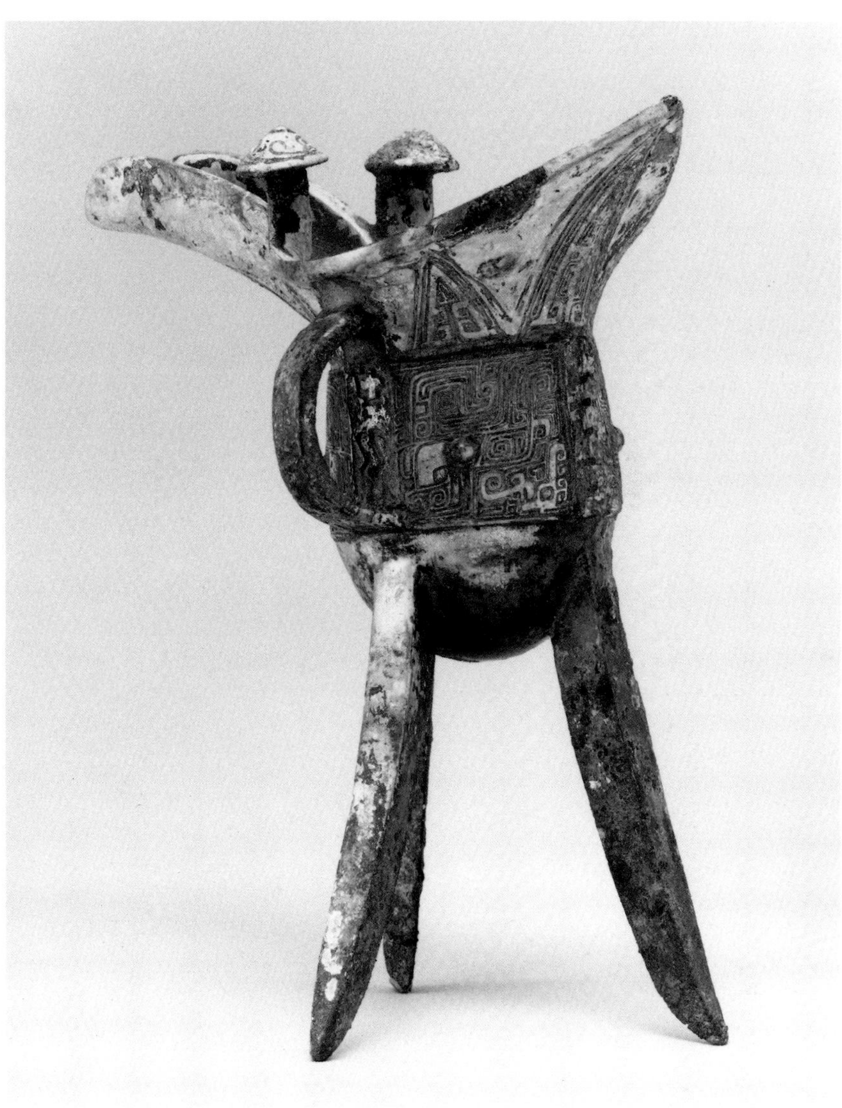

in the portrayal of these pendant dragons reveal the difficulty inherent in the clay piece-mold technique. For example, the dragon to the left of the handle is depicted with a large gaping jaw, while the dragon on the right side of the handle has no jaw and is difficult to read as anything but an abstract design.[9]

The final *jue* in this series (no. 3) dates to the late Anyang period of the Shang dynasty (late twelfth – early eleventh century B.C.) and is similar in design to no. 2; however, the proportions of this later vessel are more successful.[10] The body is longer, less squat, the legs shorter, and the spout rises at a steeper and more elegant angle. Even the two caps on the spout have a more attenuated, graceful appearance. Nevertheless, the transition between the body and the legs remains as a problem not fully resolved, and the overall appearance of the vessel is unbalanced toward the side with the handle.

Side view of the *jue* (no. 3).

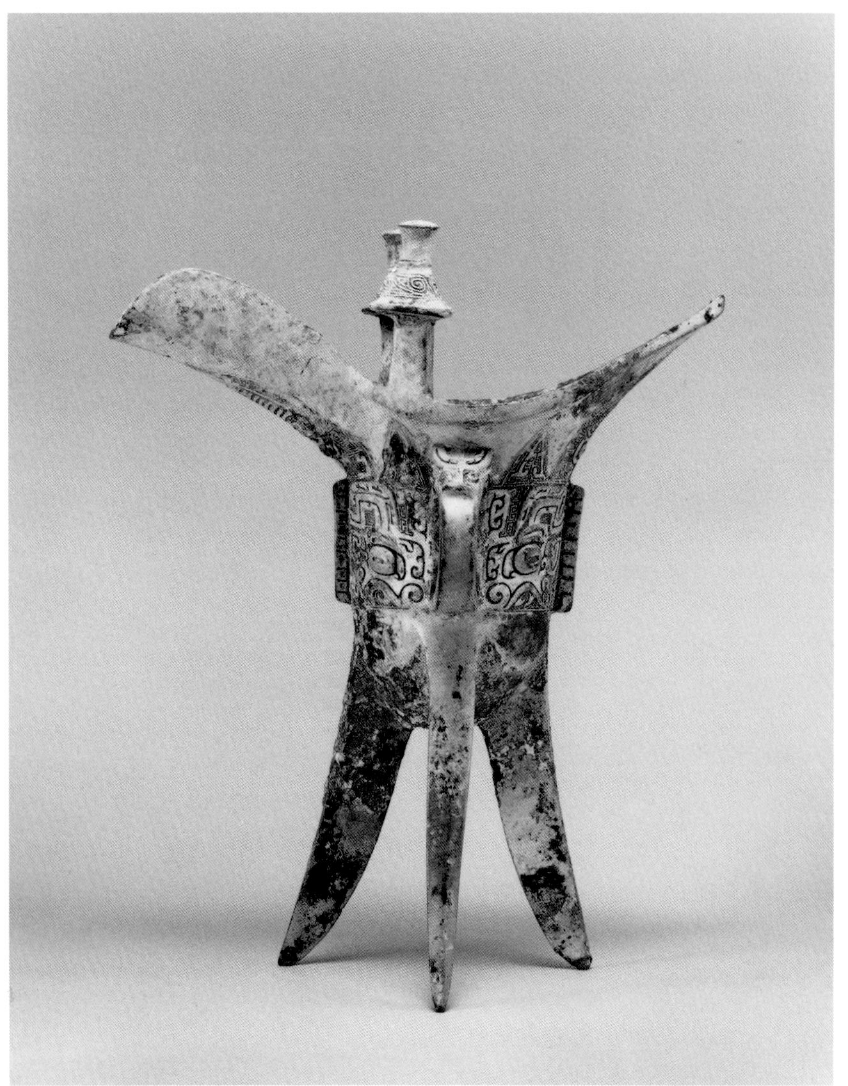

The major distinction between these two *jue* (nos. 2 and 3) lies in the clarity of the decoration on the later piece. This clarity is achieved by depicting the *taotie* mask and other major motifs with broad elements raised above the background *leiwen.* The raised curls and sharp edges of this style of decoration could not survive in ceramic, and thus reveal a fuller exploitation of the potential of bronze as a plastic medium. The *taotie* on this vessel are shown as masks without bodies: each has a gaping jaw with sharp, curved fangs; eyes with pupils; ears; and a long horn or plume. The blade-shaped designs on the spout of this vessel are decorated with cicada patterns. As with the earlier *jue* (no. 2), the area under the handle on this vessel has been filled with an inscription; an interesting addition to the handle is the head of a bovine.[11] The *leiwen* have evolved into a regular spiral pattern depicted in fine lines. It is likely that the larger motifs, such as the *taotie* and the cicada, were first carved in the model and then further refined in the mold. The sharp edges and fine detail of the *leiwen* suggest that most of it was carved in the mold.

The *guang* (no. 4) is another type of pouring vessel; it appears in the late Shang and, in contrast to the *jue,* more fully exploits the qualities of bronze. The body of this vessel, which is roughly rectangular in shape, with strong, protruding flanges at the corners, reveals a developed sensibility of the plastic qualities and durability of bronze. A similar sensibility is seen in the motifs, which are cast in the round with a variety of textures both on the surface of the vessel and on the surface of the motifs.

Like the *jue,* the *guang* has a handle, but it is at the rear rather than the side and thus does not present the problems of decoration and balance in design inherent in the *jue.* Also, the *guang* often lacks legs, which eliminates the problem of aligning the decoration with them. The *guang* usually has a tall foot and is long and narrow, with the handle and the spout at opposite ends of its long axis. There are two major sides for decoration and other opportunities for design under the spout, around the handle, and the handle itself. The vessel is designed to have a cover, which is frequently elaborately decorated and typically presents entirely different design considerations; it is missing in this example.

The decoration on the body of the *guang* is usually divided into three horizontal registers separated by undecorated bands: the upper register includes the spout and the upper handle attachment; the center register is the main body of the vessel and the lower handle attachment; and the bottom register is the foot.

This *guang* dates to the later stages of the Shang dynasty (early–mid eleventh century B.C.). As with the latest of the *jue* (no. 3), the main motifs are raised above a background of *leiwen.* On this *guang* the individual elements of the *taotie*–the horns, eyes, snout–and other elements are separated from one another by areas of *leiwen.* This slight scattering or expansion of pattern, and the continuation of the *leiwen* over the main motifs are further exploitation of the potential for elaborate three-dimensional surface decoration on bronze and indicate a later date than that of the *jue* (no. 3).

The upper section of decoration on this vessel is filled by a bird and an imaginary creature; they are divided by the side flange. The bird is shown with a hooked beak, a plume on the back of its head, and a long thin body and tail. It has been suggested that this bird is the early example of the phoenix and therefore symbolizes one of the sacred animals of the Shang.[12] An unusual creature decorates the front of the upper register; its head has a very long upper jaw with a hook on top which curls and splits at the end. There is a down-curved element in the middle of the gaping mouth and an upward-hooked lower jaw.[13]

The middle register is filled with a single *taotie* divided by the side flange. On either side of this flange are upright motifs with the nostrils of the beast at the bottom, downward-pointed hooks in the middle, and a broad pattern covered with *leiwen* at the top. This spade-shaped device has been identified as one of the elements that distinguishes the *taotie* from other composite animals on Shang bronzes.[14] Below each large eye is a gaping jaw, and above is an eyebrow and a horn. The ears are also clearly indicated but the body has been reduced to a pair of abstract patterns at the outer extremities. Both the back panel under the handle and the front panel under the spout are decorated with similar *taotie.*

The bottom register of design on this vessel consists of a pair of creatures with bodies very similar to the one with the trunk on the upper register. However, these animals have large, gaping jaws which curl out and away from each other. They have been identified as a form of dragon. Similar dragons appear on the back and front of the vessel.

An interesting motif on this *guang* is its handle. It is in the form of a beast with very large curling horns, biting the head of a bird. The surfaces of both the beast and the

Below: No. 4. *Guang*, late Shang dynasty, early–mid 11th century B.C., bronze, 7 ¼″ x 9 ½″ gift of Walter Stein, 55.209, and a drawing of the inscription on the base.

Opposite: No. 5. *Ding*, late Shang dynasty, early–mid 11th century B.C., 9 ½″ x 8 ⅜″ gift of Mrs. Donald E. Frederick, 49.152

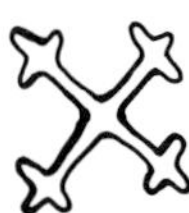

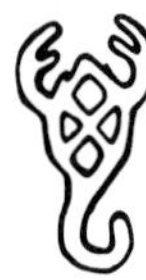

bird are extensively decorated: the neck of the beast has scales, while the bird has large protruding eyes, a hooked beak, C-shaped wings, claws, and a long tail indicated against a ground of *leiwen* on each side.[15]

Vessels for the ritual preparation and serving of food do not have some of the design requirements found in wine vessels and thus present different forms and decorative schemes. Food was generally served from these vessels with ladles; making handles, spouts, and forms to accommodate pouring unnecessary. Therefore, food vessels tend to be somewhat simpler and provide an easier surface for the application of the symmetrical designs of the early Bronze Age than contemporary wine vessels. The most common food vessel is the *ding,* which has two basic shapes, round and rectangular. This round *ding* (no. 5) is roughly contemporary with the latest of the *jue* (no. 3) and the *guang* (no. 4).

Faint vertical lines through the decoration indicate that this *ding* was cast in a three-part mold separated along the flanges that align with the legs and visually mark the edges of the units of decoration. Thus, each

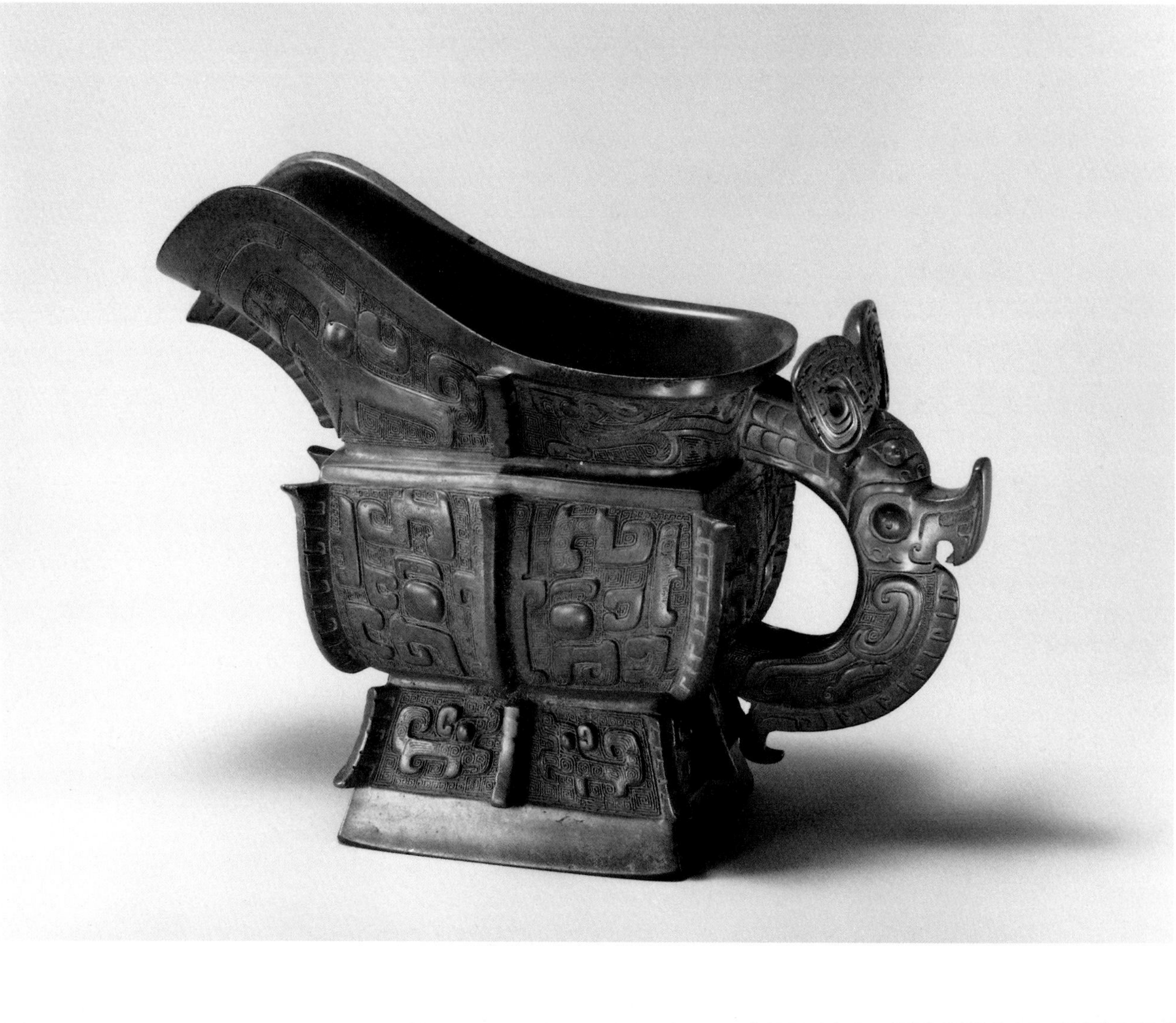

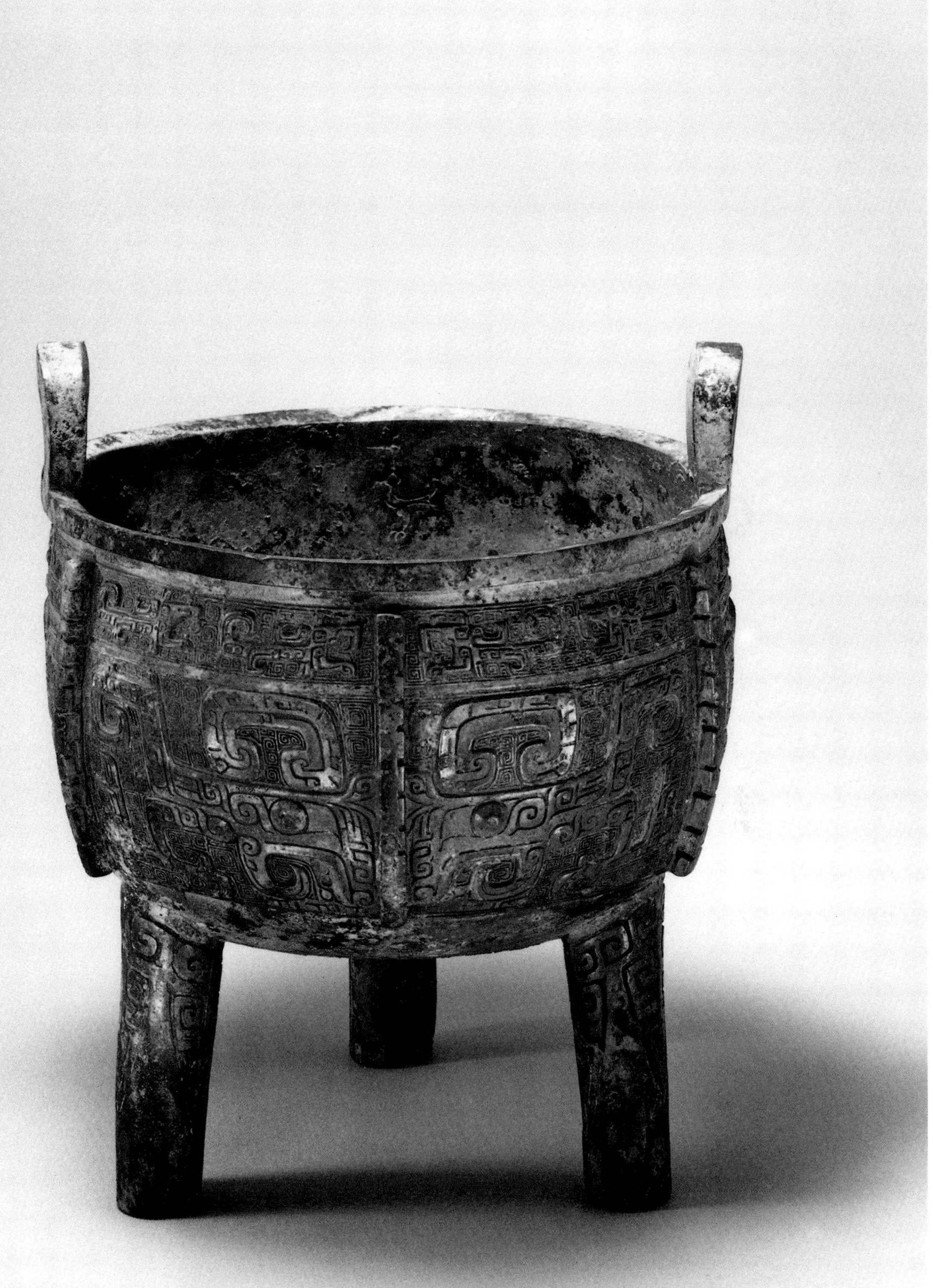

of the three units would have filled one section of the mold. Slight overflows indicate that the body of this vessel was cast first, the molds for the lugs and the legs were then attached, and these elements were cast onto the body. In the absence of soldering, welding, or brazing, which came much later, the development of the rather cumbersome techniques of casting elements onto a vessel or precasting these elements and casting the vessel onto them allowed for the addition of handles, legs, and other elaborate appendages that were impossible to create in one casting in a piece mold. This freed the bronze casters from the closed form dictated by the piece-mold process and vastly increased their repertoire of three-dimensional decoration.

Similar to those on the *jue* (no. 3), the major decorative motifs on this *ding* are raised and displayed against a background of *leiwen.*[16] The comparative simplicity of applying decoration to the *ding* is amply evident in this piece. The design is divided into three distinct large areas by the three flanges aligned with the legs; each area is bisected by an intermediate flange that is decorative rather than deriving from the mold structure. The three-part symmetry of the vessel permits it to be dealt with in design terms as one unit with no conflict among function, form, and decoration. The only inconsistency with the three-part scheme occurs with the two lugs on the rim.

Each of the three units of decoration on this vessel is divided horizontally into two bands, which are divided vertically by the intermediate flange. The larger band of decoration is filled with two flange-divided halves of the *taotie,* which has a broad snout and mouth opened to reveal several teeth and a hooked lower jaw, large curling horns, a short body with a curling tail, and a single pair of legs with elaborate plumes. The spade-shaped device found in the middle of many *taotie* at the forehead level does not appear in this example.[17] The upper register of design consists of two pairs of mirror-image creatures presented in profile and divided by the flange. Unlike the *taotie,* these creatures have down-hooked beaks, up-curled plumes at the back of the head, long, thin bodies with up-curled tails, and what appear to be three legs, the front one lifted to create the impression that they are trotting along in their register in processions that confront each other at the flange.[18] The sense of dynamic yet contained motion suggested in these motifs contrasts with the largely static and balanced designs on earlier vessels and indicates the increased sophistication of the bronze caster and of the culture in which he lived. Blade motifs similar to those found in the upper register of design on the *jue* (no. 3) decorate the legs of this vessel. Inside the vessel near the lip is a single-character inscription which has the form of an ax and a bird.

The rectangular *ding* or *fang ding* (no. 6) is a shape that has no direct prototypes in ceramics and reveals the extent to which bronze casting had evolved from its Neolithic predecessors by the late Shang dynasty. A rectangular form, particularly one like this *fang ding,* which has flanges on each of the four corners, presents numerous abrupt edges that were impractical in a fragile medium like ceramic. The seams that join the four sides and flat base also present structural weaknesses in ceramic that were not an issue in a cast vessel. The delicately curled flanges on this vessel are a motif that could not have survived in ceramic.

The *fang ding* is generally cast in a four-part mold, one part corresponding to each side. It has four major areas of decoration, one on each side of the vessel; these areas are flat, rectangular, and are not affected by

Opposite: No. 6 *Fang ding,* late Shang dynasty, early–mid 11th century B.C., 8 ½″ x 6 ¾,″ Margaret E. Fuller Purchase Fund, 54.177

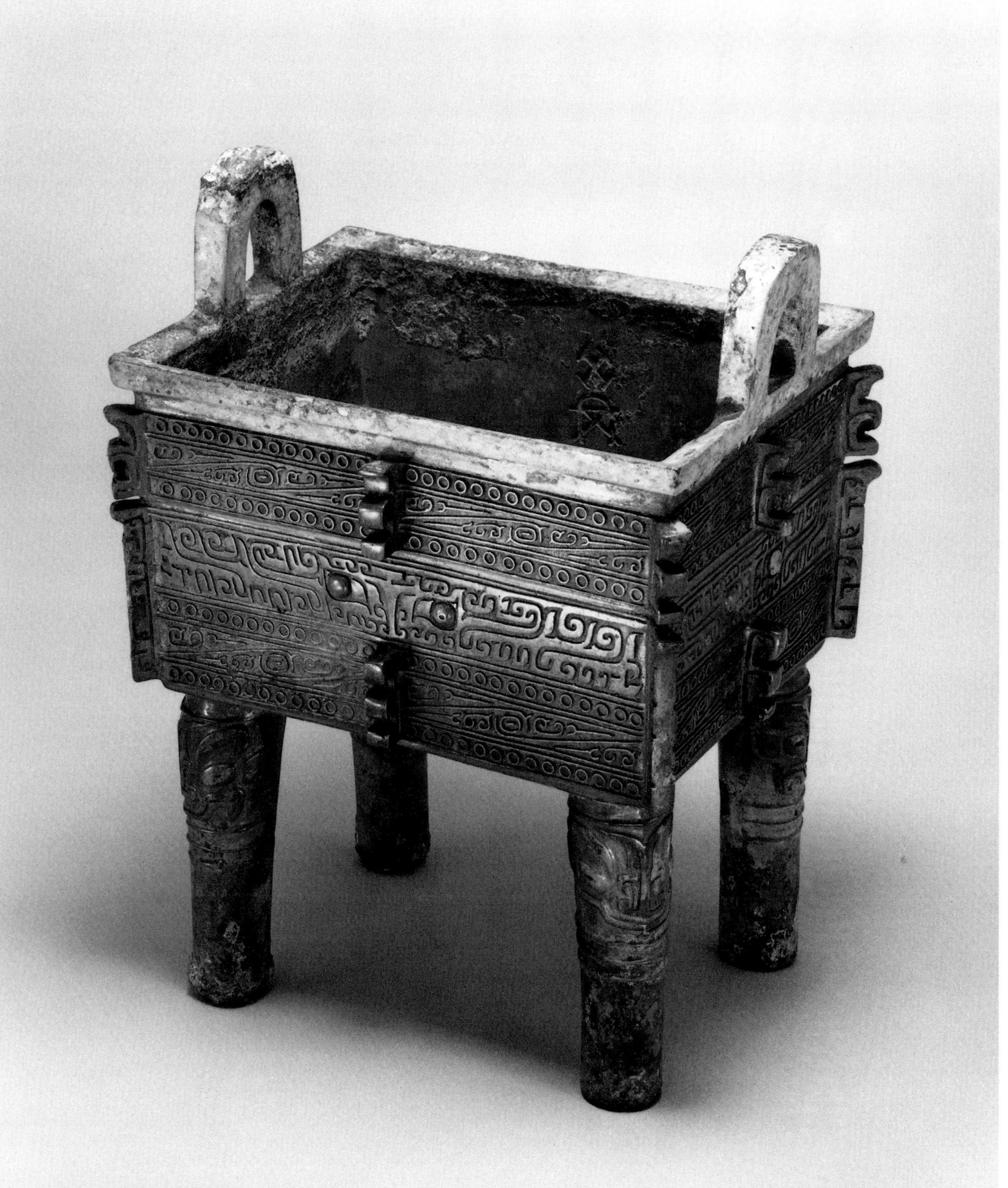

mold lines. Therefore, the *fang ding* presented an ideal surface for the presentation of the symmetrically arranged decoration of the period. The decoration on this *fang ding* is similar to that on the earliest of the *jue* (no. 1), except that the *ding* has three registers, the upper and lower in thread relief and the central register in broader elements. The high degree of finish, the presence of the flanges and the large masks on the legs indicate a much later date for this vessel, at the very end of the Shang dynasty (early–mid eleventh century B.C.). This type of design is also known in a number of vessels dating from Western Zhou. The intentionally archaistic approach of this vessel indicates sophistication, both in the culture for which it was produced and in the technical and artistic capabilities of those who created it. It seems possible that the motifs seen on earlier Shang ritual vessels were losing their significance by this point, and that the designs on this vessel serve a largely decorative purpose. The upper and lower registers are purely abstract, with only the central band maintaining the *taotie* motif.[19]

The *gui,* like the *ding,* is a food vessel; its prototype is to be found in the footed ceramic vessels of the Neolithic period. This type of round vessel was made with or without handles. Like the typical *guang,* the *gui* has a ring foot rather than legs; in some examples a tall, square base is attached to the ring foot.

The earliest *gui* illustrated here (no. 7) dates to the mid second millennium B.C., roughly contemporary with the second *jue* (no. 2). Cast in a three-part mold, the *gui* reveals both a strong reference to its ceramic prototype and to the growing consciousness of the decorative and structural characteristics of bronze. The link to the ceramic prototype is to be seen in the closed, round form. An increased interest in surface, visi-

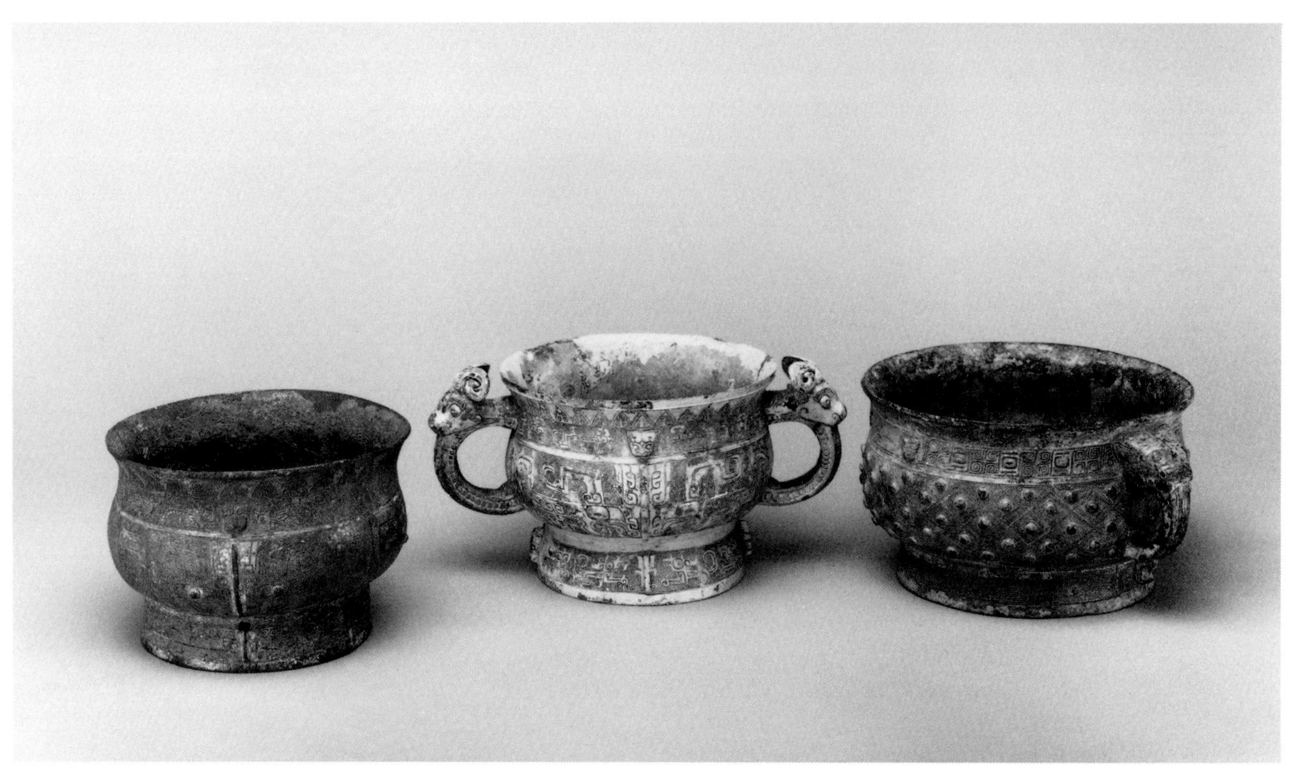

Left to right: No. 7 *Gui,* Shang dynasty, mid second millennium B.C., 4 ⅞″ x 7 ⅜,″ Thomas D. Stimson Memorial Collection, 45.48; No. 8. *Gui,* Shang dynasty, early–mid 11th century B.C., 5 ⅜″ x 10 ¾,″ Margaret E. Fuller Purchase Fund, 56.34; No. 9. *Gui,* early Western Zhou dynasty, mid 11th–10th century B.C., 5 ⅛″ x 10 ½,″ Thomas D. Stimson Memorial Collection, 48.183

ble in the flanges and in the overall decorative scheme, reveals the concerns of the bronze worker of this period.

The decoration on this vessel is divided into three registers, a minor band encircling the eversion of the lip, a major band covering the body, and another minor band around the foot. As in most handleless *gui,* the decoration is repeated three times around the vessel's circumference. Mold lines occur at the divisions of the decoration areas, indicating that each unit of design was carved into one section of the three-part mold. Flanges divide the *taotie* but do not occur at the mold lines, suggesting that the flanges are used purely as decoration and do not serve a structural function. Although a form of flange appeared on certain ceramics of the Neolithic period, the elaborate and carefully sculpted versions that appear on this vessel are a bronze form.

The lip decoration band has two sections; one consists of a series of blade-shaped devices that reach to the lip. The lower section is arranged around three medallionlike bovine heads with inverted C-shaped horns, diamond-shaped motifs in the middle of the forehead, and broad snouts. A pair of birds faces the bovine head on either side. These birds are depicted on a background of *leiwen;* they are on the same plain as the *leiwen* but are distinguished by being developed in much broader lines. Each bird has a round head and eye, an inordinately large hooked beak, claws, wings, and a long tail covered with scalelike motifs.

The middle band covering the swelling of the bowl is decorated with the *taotie,* which is also depicted in broader elements on a background of *leiwen.* The *taotie* is divided by a nonstructural flange. On either side of the flange is a broad motif that is spade-shaped at the top and is the snout of the beast at the bottom. The beast has large, inverted C-shaped horns, an inwardly hooked jaw, and a thin body with a down-hooked tail. The single leg is bent back and ends in a claw. Under the tail is a small zoomorph which appears to be a cross between a bird and a dragon. This beast has a hooked beak similar to the bird on the top register of design, a long claw, and a short tail that ends perilously close to the claw of the *taotie.*

The main motif on the lowest register of decoration on this vessel's foot is also a *taotie.* Unlike the one on the main band, it is depicted in relatively thin lines, with a simple spade-shaped device flanking the flange. It has an outward- rather than inward-hooked jaw. The horn on this *taotie* is a double spiral that is distinguished from the double spiral of the *leiwen* only by the width of the lines. A badly corroded inscription appears in the bottom of the inside of this vessel.

The second *gui* (no. 8) in this series dates to the late Shang dynasty (early–mid eleventh century B.C.) Although retaining the traditional shape of the *gui,* this vessel reveals the level the late Shang dynasty bronze caster had reached in mastering his medium. This is particularly evident in the exuberantly sculpted handles and in the raised decoration.

Typical of the *gui* with handles, the overall decoration is repeated twice on this vessel, once on each side of the bowl.[20] This contrasts with the handleless *gui* on which the decoration is usually repeated three times. Like the *gui* just discussed (no. 7), the designs on this vessel are divided into three horizontal registers, with minor ones on the lip and foot and the major register in the middle. Mold lines under one handle and through each of the *taotie* indicate these two units of decoration were executed in a three-part mold and must have been

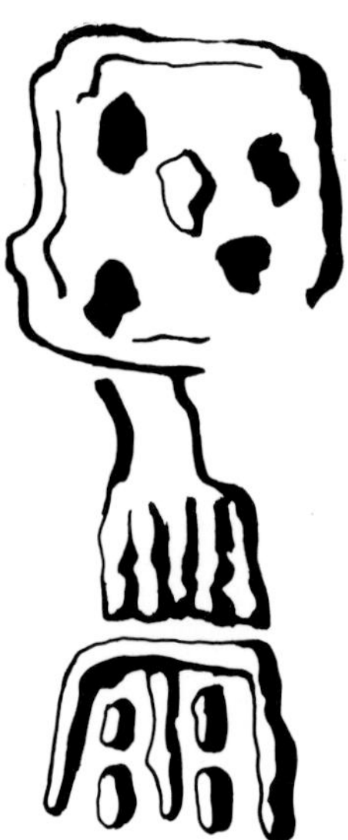

applied first to the model, then refined in the mold.

The top of the upper register has blade-shaped devices similar to those of no. 7, but in this case they end at a clearly marked line below the rim. The top register is decorated with two pairs of beasts on either side, each pair facing a central bovine head. Like those on the previous *gui*, the heads on this vessel have inverted C-shaped horns, diamond-shaped bosses in the middle of their foreheads, and broad snouts. The beasts that face them also have inverted C-shaped horns; as well as outward-curved snouts and lower jaws, hooks on their backs, single legs, and upward-curled tails. These creatures are known as *kui* dragons.

The center register has the now-familiar *taotie* divided by a flange. Flanking the flange is the spade-shaped motif. The horns are very long, and each has an additional upward hook that suggests a plume. The large eyes have deeply cut pupils and are flanked by evenly striated ears. The lower jaw is inwardly hooked, and there are a number of particularly nasty looking teeth on the upper jaw. The creature has a single leg and a downward-hooked tail. Between this creature and the handles is a pair of pendant dragons that stretch the full width of the register. They have two legs, upcurled snouts, inward-hooked lower jaws, and straight tails.

The lower register is also divided by a

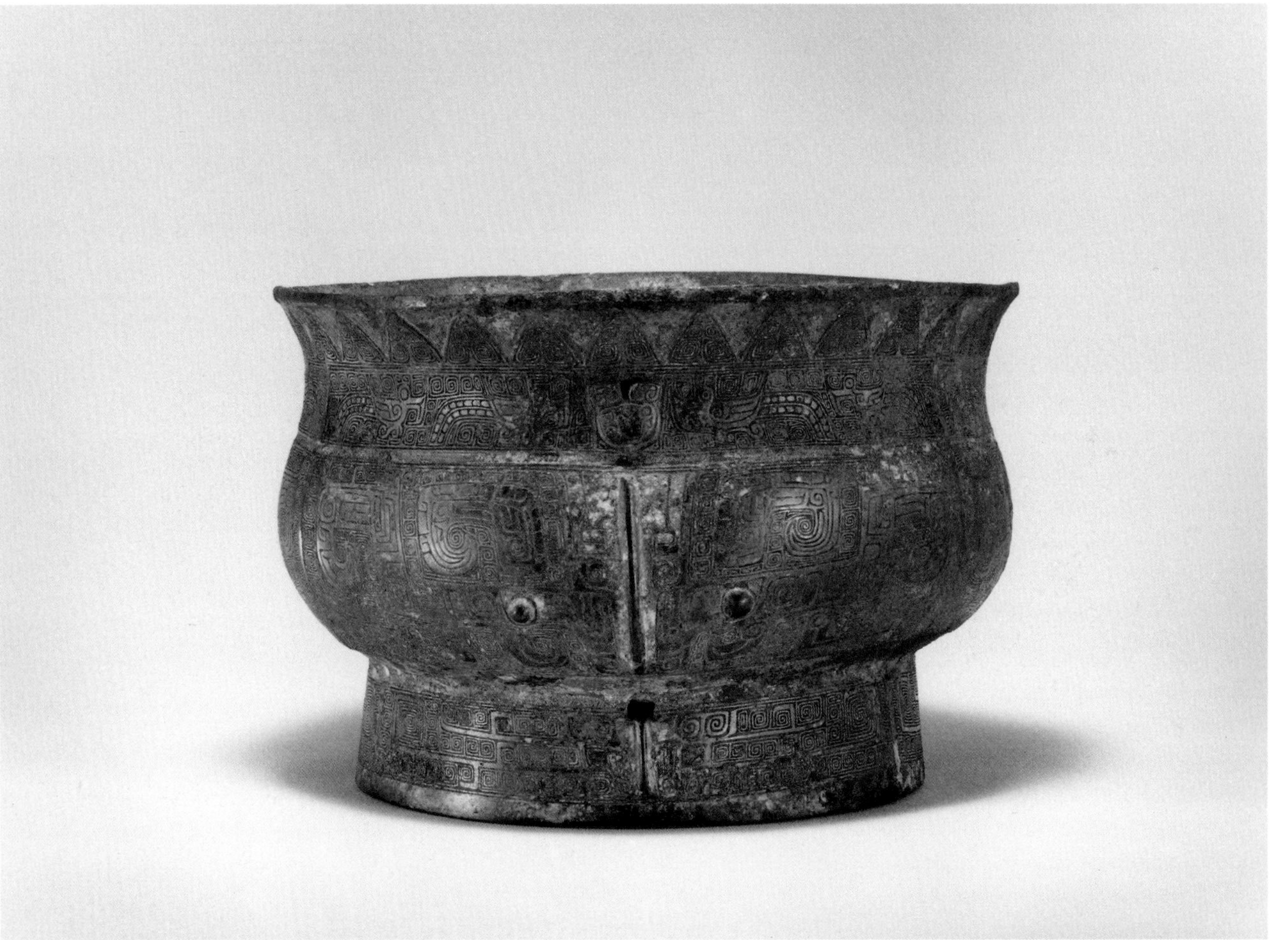

flange, and flanking this flange is a spade-shaped device similar to that in the center of the *taotie.* This device is repeated with, as well as without, the *taotie* a number of times on this vessel and on others, and was either a stock part of the decorative vocabulary of the time, or had some particular significance. Facing this device on either side are pairs of the birdlike creatures that also appeared on the bottom register of the *ding* (no. 5).

The third *gui* (no. 9) dates to the early Western Zhou dynasty (mid eleventh–tenth century B.C.) and presents an entirely different approach to the problems of surface decoration.[21] As with the other two *gui* discussed here, the decoration is divided into three registers and, like other *gui* with handles, is repeated twice. Vertical mold marks through the center of each unit of design and under the handles indicate that this vessel was made in a four-part mold.

The surface designs on this *gui* are almost completely abstract. Each of the two decorative units of the upper register is divided at the center by a bovine head similar in form to those that appear on nos. 7 and 8. The remainder of the decoration consists of a band formed by groups of four spirals in a rectangular frame alternating with oval motifs, which are obviously derived from the eye shapes seen in the *taotie* on earlier vessels. The center register is made up of a series of diamond-shaped motifs filled with

Opposite: *Gui* (no. 7) and a drawing of the inscription on the interior bottom.

Below: *Gui* (no. 8).

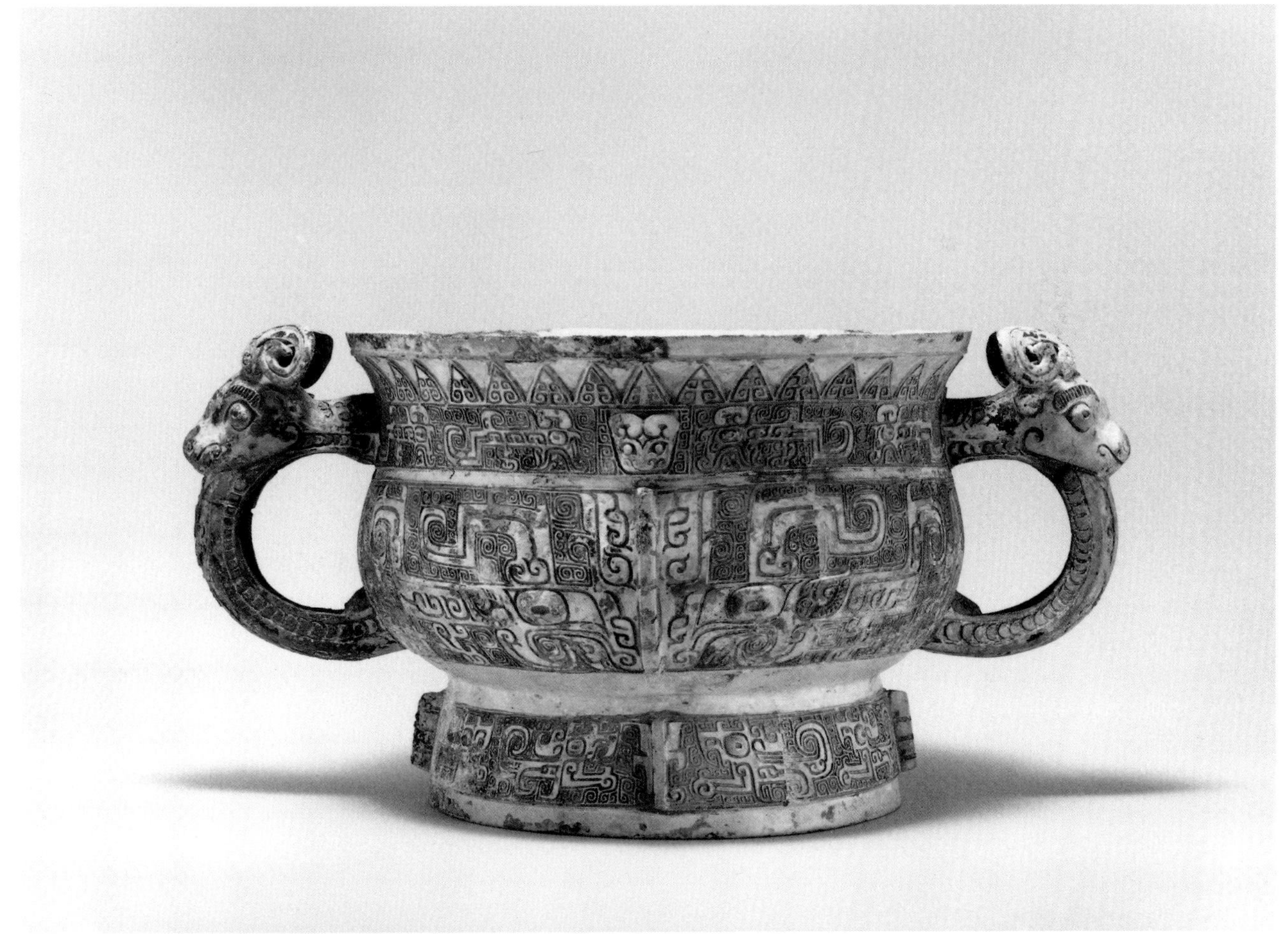

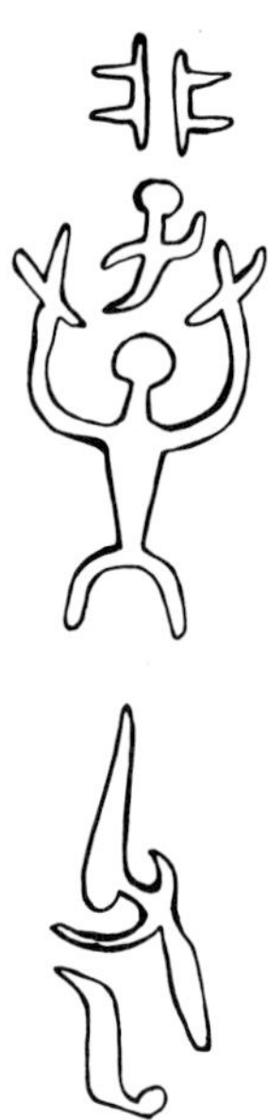

squared spirals and bosses. Positioned point to point, these motifs create a continuous frieze. This type of pattern is unusual on vessels other than *gui* and *ding*. The earliest examples occur on vessels of the early Anyang period.[22]

The lower register is also abstract, but in finer patterns than the upper register. This register is divided into a series of rectangles that contain elements recognizable as parts of a *taotie;* they are arranged symmetrically on either side of a central "eye." Some scattering or expansion of motifs has been seen in vessels discussed above and continues to be a major factor in decoration during the Western Zhou.

The handles on this vessel begin with heads that have the horns, eyes, and snout of a buffalo or other bovine. However, their mouths are filled with sharp teeth that appear to bite the dependent handle. The outer surfaces of these handles are decorated with three spade-shaped devices; each ends in a hooked flange. The handles appear to have been cast onto this vessel, but unlike the handles on no. 7, the casting is very precise, with only minimal overflows. The area under the handle is slightly raised, the bosses of the middle register of design have been removed, and a slightly different pattern has been applied, indicating that the area under the handle was part of the same, separate casting as the handles.

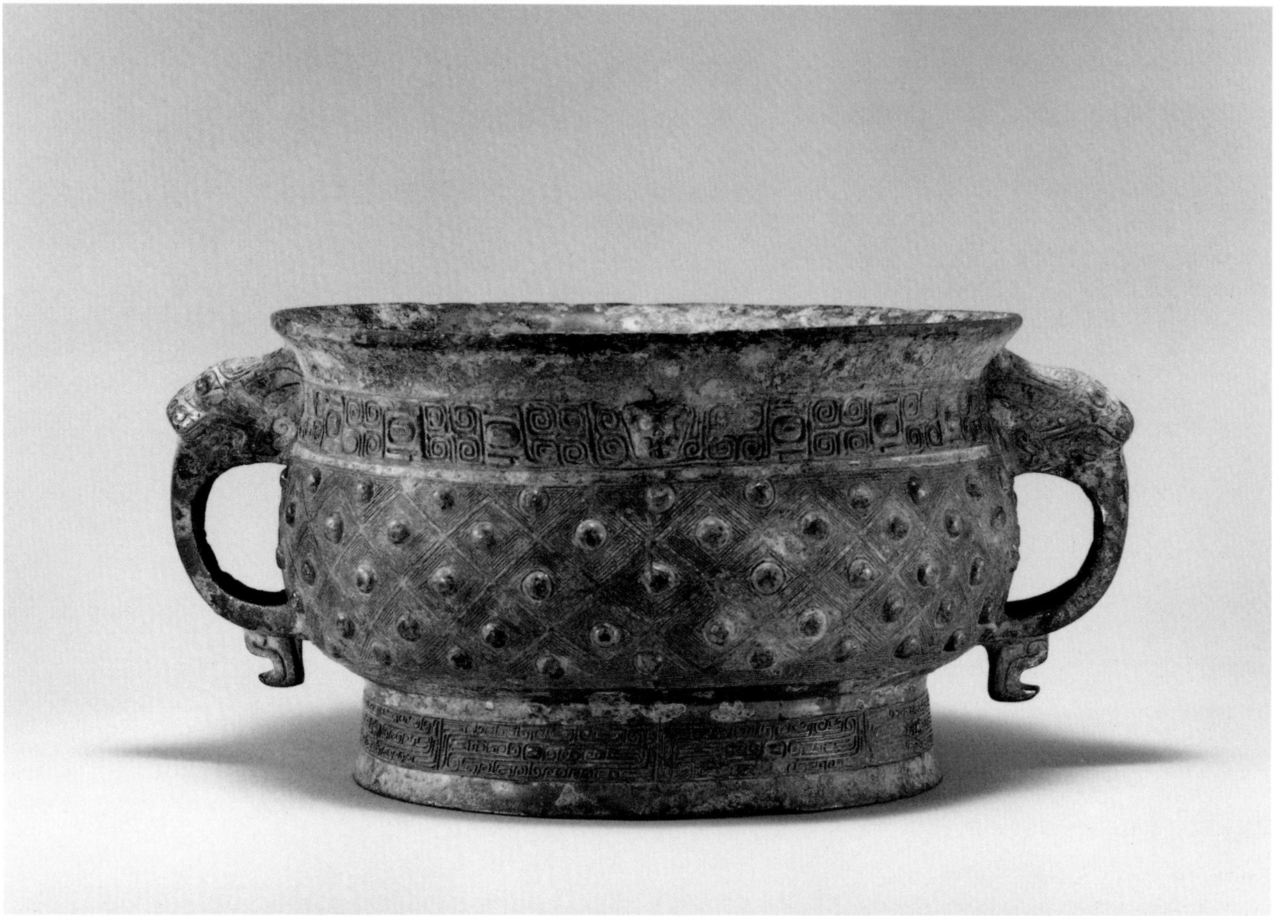

The basic issues addressed by the bronze caster of the Shang dynasty were divorcing his craft from its ceramic prototypes and exploring the full decorative and structural potential of his medium. In structure and form vessels evolved from the often asymmetrical but closed designs of ceramics to shapes in which the characteristics of bronze were more fully realized. This is apparent in the three *jue,* which evolved from an almost clumsy, asymmetrical form to as coherent a statement as it was possible to obtain within the tradition of the vessel type. The introduction of rectangular vessels such as the *fang ding* (no. 6) and of elaborately sculpted handles such as those on the *gui* (no. 9) are also examples of a developing awareness of the structural characteristics of bronze.

Decoration evolved as artisans experimented with the two opportunities their technique presented for adding surface designs: creating the model and refining the mold. Designs advanced from simple linear motifs perhaps borrowed from decoration on Neolithic jades to raised and curled designs executed in full relief as is strikingly evident in the *guang* (no. 4). By the end of the Shang dynasty, many of these structural and decorative issues had been resolved, allowing for quite different developments in the periods that followed.

Opposite: *Gui* (no. 9) and a drawing of the inscription on the interior bottom.

II: The Western Zhou Dynasty and Spring and Autumn Period

Below: Drawing of the inscription on both the interior lid and the interior bottom of the *you* (no. 10).

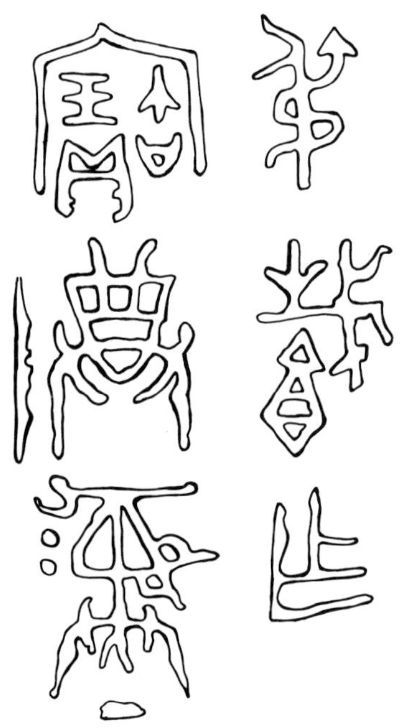

Opposite: No. 10. *You,* Western Zhou dynasty, mid 11th–10th century B.C., 9 3⁄8″ x 8″, Eugene Fuller Memorial Collection, 51.67

The Shang dynasty fell to the Zhou in the early to mid eleventh century B.C.[23] The Zhou dynasty ruled by a feudal system, appointing family members or meritorious subjects to control areas as lords of various ranks. This system was successful as long as the central Zhou government remained powerful and loyalty of the lords to the Zhou remained stronger than their regional interests. However, by the early eighth century B.C., a decline in the Zhou allowed for and, in part, was caused by an increase in regionalism. By 772 B.C. the Zhou dynasty had declined to the extent that invading armies were able to attack and defeat it. Much weakened, the Zhou government moved its capital east to an area near the modern city of Luoyang; this event marked the end of the Western Zhou (c. mid eleventh century–772 B.C.) and the beginning of the Eastern Zhou (771–220 B.C.). The collapse of the dominant Zhou culture permitted the rise of regional tendencies in religion, culture, and the arts, and these tendencies were the dominant factor of the early part of the Eastern Zhou dynasty, known as the Spring and Autumn period.

The Zhou rulers followed ritual practices influenced by, but with an emphasis different from, those of the Shang. Ritual bronzes continued to be produced in large numbers, but inscriptions are more frequent, much longer, and different in content; they are often secular, indicating that the ritual significance of the vessels was declining. Whereas the majority of Shang dynasty ritual vessels were used for serving wine, most Zhou vessels were used for serving food. The motifs familiar from Shang bronzes begin to vanish during the Western Zhou, adding to the series of technical, structural, and design issues that arose as new schemes appeared to fulfill altered ritual function and decorative preference. Some of this change has already been seen in the *fang ding* (no. 6) and the *gui* (no. 9).[24]

The *you* (no. 10) is a vessel type that appeared in the Shang dynasty and remained popular in the Western Zhou. Used to serve liquids, this vessel had a bail handle and a cover. When removed, the cover can serve as a cup, its top ring inverted to become a foot and the two protrusions acting as handles. The oval cross-section of the body of the *you* presented two sides for decoration and allowed for casting in a two-part mold. However, the ring foot and flat bottom required an additional mold section. Thus, the experimentation seen in mold design during the late Shang continued in the Western Zhou. The overall appearance of this vessel is in striking contrast to vessels of the late Shang. Gone are the sharp protruding elements, elaborate surface decoration, and rigid profiles. A Western Zhou preference for softer, smoother forms is seen in the swelling body of this vessel, with its relatively low center of gravity; an appreciation of the qualities inherent in bronze–its sheen, its color, and general appearance–is apparent in the broad undecorated expanses on this and many other vessels of this period.

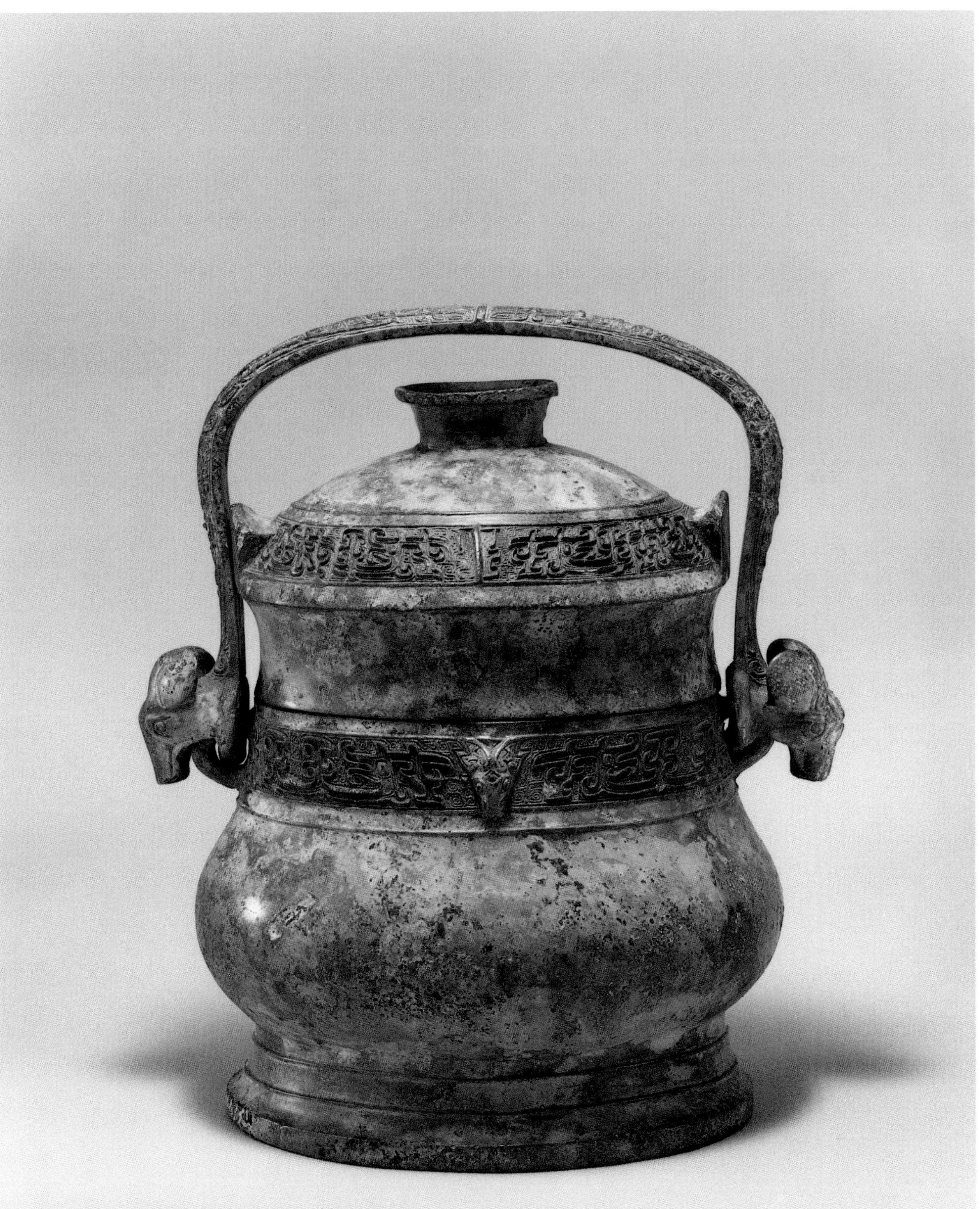

20

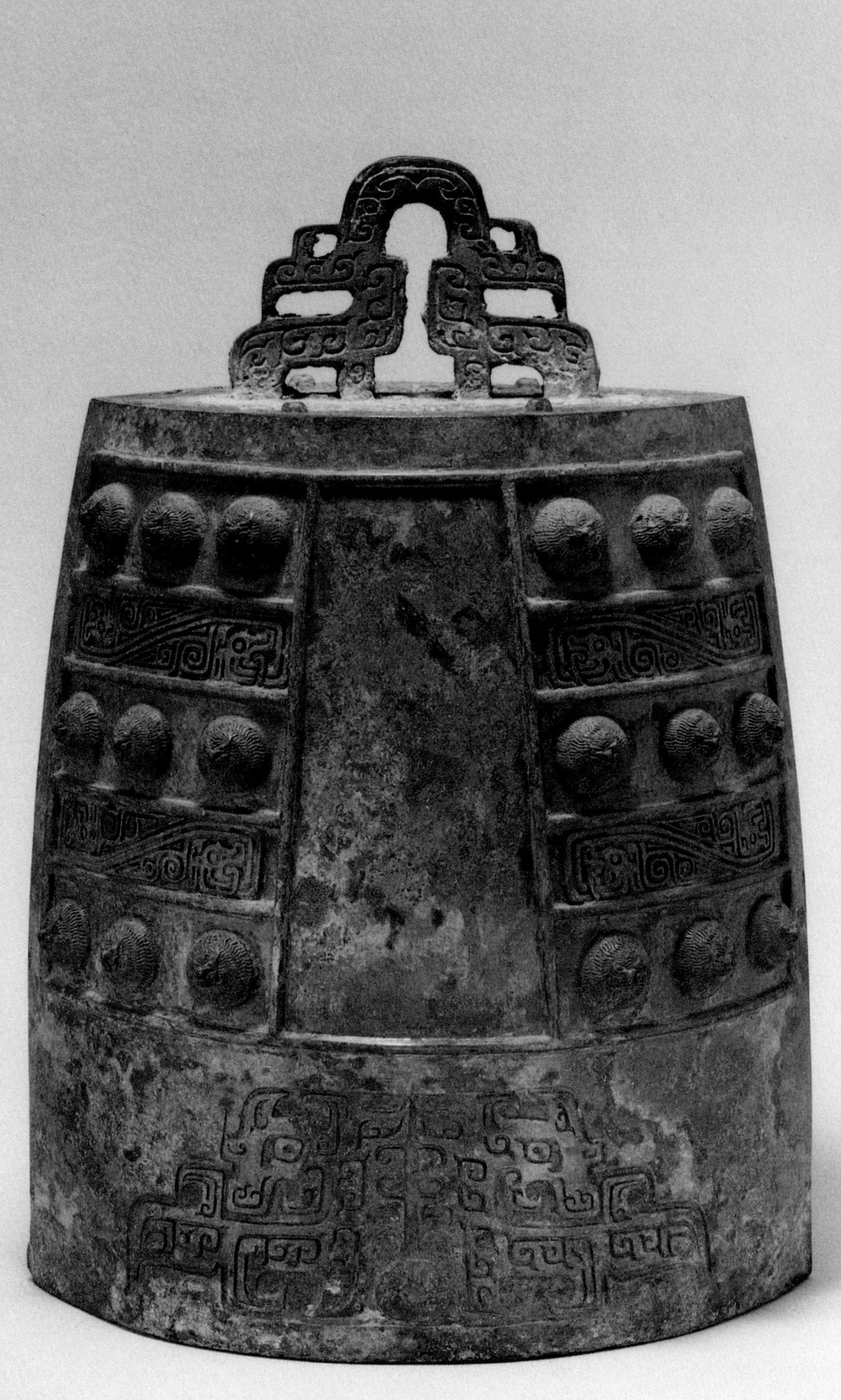

The trend toward abstraction seen in the late Shang *fang ding* (no. 6) and the Western Zhou *gui* (no. 9) is also present in the *you.* The decoration of this vessel is limited to two narrow bands, one located near the top of the body and the other on the lid; much more elaborate decoration appears on the handle. The two bands of decoration consist of *taotie* depicted in very thin raised lines against a background of *leiwen.* On the lid are four pairs of these motifs, two on each side. These *taotie* have plumes attached to the backs of their heads; the heads are twisted to look back over the bodies; the bodies are long and end in elaborate tails. In the band on the body of the vessel, the body but not the head of the dragon is repeated directly from this tail; on the upper band, two pairs of complete dragons are depicted on each side. The repetition of the headless dragon's body on the vessel is interesting, particularly since space was left near the attachment point of the handles to add pendant dragons. Obviously, the sanctity of the motif was no longer of great importance; in later pieces it is common to see a headless body or a pair of bodies with one head repeated as the main design. The handle of the vessel ends in two ram's heads, the remainder is decorated with two pairs of cicadas with long feelers, depicted against a ground of *leiwen.*

This *you* indicates other shifts in attitude toward decoration on Western Zhou vessels. For example, the motif that separates the pairs of dragons on the handle is similar in shape to the motif that forms the center part of the *taotie* on the *guang* (no. 4). On the *you* it appears independently, whereas on the *guang* it is a major component of the *taotie.* Heads of recognizable animals, which had begun to appear in increasing numbers during the late Shang, are routine on vessels of the Western Zhou. The spectacular pair of rams terminating the handles and the animals with broad palmate horns marking the center of the body bands demonstrate this shift.

During the Western Zhou, several varieties of ritual bells took their final forms and presented a series of unique technological and decorative issues. These bells were one of a number of ritual implements popular throughout China during the Western and Eastern Zhou that, although regional tendencies are apparent in surface decoration, were relatively consistent in shape. Zhou dynasty bells were suspended by their handles from a frame and were divided into four sections: suspension (*yong* or *niu*), flat area around the top of the bell (*wu*), upper section of the body of the bell (*zheng*), which is further divided into decorative bands (*zhuan*) and bosses (*mei*), and lower section of the bell (*gu*), which is divided into the projections at the end of the rim (*xian*), the decorative panel in the center (*dui* or *sui*), and the rim (*yu*). The bells were played by striking the bottom section with a wooden mallet or pole; each bell produced two notes, one when struck on the *xian* and the second when struck on the *dui.* By the late Western Zhou, these two notes were generally separated by a major third and were produced by the physics of the oval cross-section of the bell. Sets of bells ranged in number from five to as many as sixty-four. The difference in notation from bell to bell was determined by size: the smaller the bell, the higher the two notes it produced.

The precision required to produce the correct notes in these bells must have presented a formidable challenge to the metalsmiths of this period. The oval cross-section permitted the body of the bell to be cast in a two-part mold. However, like the ring foot and flat bottom of the *you,* the flat top and suspension system of the bell required the addition of one or more sections to the

Opposite: No. 11. *Bo zhong,* Eastern Zhou dynasty, early to mid Spring and Autumn period, late 7th–early 6th century B.C., 15 3/8″ x 10 3/4″, purchased with funds from the Asian Art Council of the Seattle Art Museum and friends, the Margaret E. Fuller Purchase Fund, and the Eugene Fuller Memorial Collection by exchange to honor Henry Trubner, Senior Curator Emeritus, 87.43

Below: Detail of the bosses (no. 11).

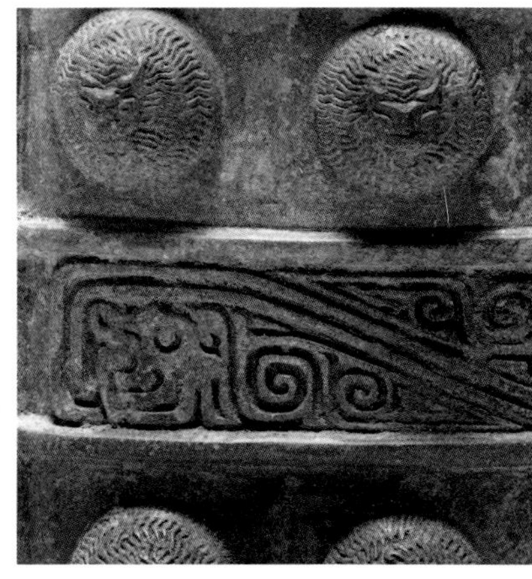

mold. The size and thickness of the body of the bell, the length of the *mei,* and the overall composition of the design had to be carefully controlled to create the correct notes. Special areas where bronze could be removed to adjust the sound were located inside the bell.

Function generally dictated the form and decoration of the bell. To avoid interfering with the playing surface and to allow for proper tuning, raised decoration appears only on the *wu, zheng,* and *dui* sections. Except for the *mei,* which influences the duration of the note and the range of overtones, and the suspension system, which does not directly influence the sound of the bell, this decoration is limited to low relief or intaglio. The decoration on this large flat-bottomed bell (*bo zhong,* no. 11) is largely abstract but retains recognizable shapes: the loop suspension (*niu*) is in the form of two plumed birds or felines; the bosses (*mei*) are decorated with curling lines and end in small masks; the bands (*zhuan*) are decorated with pairs of dragons as are the panels (*dui*). The dragons on the *dui* face away from one another and have a small disk between them. Stylistic comparison with similar examples from datable tombs places this piece in the late seventh to early sixth century B.C.

This *bo,* the largest of a group of nine found in Luoyang by Bishop White, is an example of the style that persevered at the Zhou capital during the early Eastern Zhou.[25] Although in a much reduced status from the peak of its power in the Western Zhou, the Zhou state retained prestige and influence during the early decades of this period. The formality and dignity of form and decoration of this piece are elements that appear in the somewhat conservative styles of the capital of this declining dynasty.

Although regional foundries of varying size proliferated during the late Western and early Eastern Zhou, archaeological evidence indicates that certain foundries were large in scale and provided bronze ritual vessels, weapons, tools, and other implements to broad geographic areas. The exchange of materials from such foundries as booty from warfare, or through the developing market economy of the time, was one factor that led to some consistency in styles during this period of increased regionalism. The remains of the enormous foundry of the state of Jin at Houma in Shanxi province indicate that this was one such center. The remains of large-scale mining at Tonglushan in Hubei province indicate that another foundry might have existed near that site.[26]

An example of a type of bronze design associated with the foundries at Houma is this harness buckle (no. 12). Its base is formed of a ring with three struts in the center. The ring is decorated with a series of dragons that appear to be intertwined, the neck of one going over the body of the next. These dragons have large gaping mouths and no legs; their bodies are decorated with a row of raised dots. The three struts in the middle of the ring are decorated with three parallel lines connected by diagonal striations. The intertwined dragon and variety of surface textures are elements common to bronzes from Houma.

The top section of the buckle is even more diverse in textures and surfaces. It begins at the front with a beast with a long-snouted head and a split body that forms a rectangle. The idea of the animal with a split body, heretofore drawn in one plane, emerges in three dimensions in this beast. The head and the body of this animal are covered with rows of dots. A fantastic tortoise seizes and bites the body of this beast. This tortoise has big eyes and ears, three claws, a head covered with hatched patterns, legs with dots, and a neck with scales which have dots in the center. Its shell is covered with scale patterns and is rimmed with smaller, more densely packed, but similar devices. The body and rear legs are covered with small dots, while the tail is decorated with more linear patterns. Looping across the back of the tortoise is a snake covered with dots in three parallel rows. The body of the snake forms a second rectangle corresponding with that of the snouted beast, with its tail on one side of the tortoise and its head on the other. The snake is firmly held by the rear claws of the tortoise. The combined snake and tortoise were very important in the Western Han and later mythology as the symbol for the direction north. Whether this iconography had begun to develop as early as this buckle is open to conjecture.

Interlaced designs and a fascinating variety of surface textures are qualities associated with the bronzes of northern China during this period and are very common in the mold remains found at Houma. The regional style at Houma was affected by its proximity to the conservative center of the Zhou state and also to new motifs and styles derived from contact with the nomadic people to the north and west of China. The appearance of interlace and a range of surface textures is frequently described as a result of nomadic contact. The theme of animal combat was also popular in the arts of these nomadic people and may have influenced the relationship among the various beasts on this buckle.

Horses played an important role in the status of the Shang and Zhou aristocracy, and

No. 12. Harness buckle, late Spring and Autumn period–early Warring States period, 6th–5th century B.C., 4 ⅛" x 5 ¾," Eugene Fuller Memorial Collection, 51.93

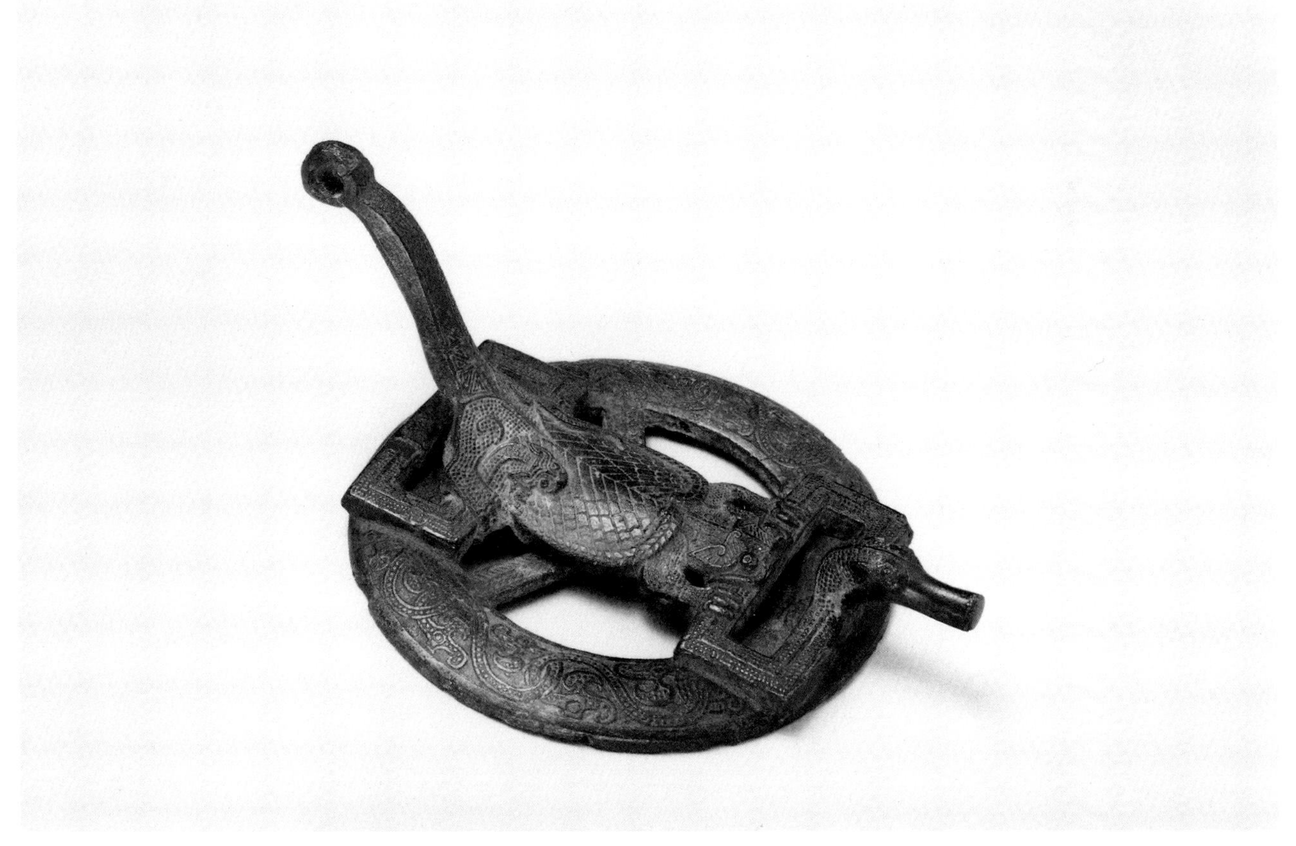

the ritual interment of horses is frequent in the burials of this period. At that time, horses were used to pull chariots and were not ridden; harnesses with multiple buckles attached the horses to the chariot. Numbers of entire chariots with horses in full harness were included in the chariot pits that accompany the tombs of the Zhou aristocracy; this harness buckle must have come from such a burial. It reveals an application of new techniques to solve the problems inherent in creating a functional buckle. This buckle has two points for attaching lines or straps: the loop in the tail of the tortoise in the rear, and the head of the beast at the front. It is designed to allow a strap to pass through the gap between the snake and the tortoise at the back, between the upper and lower pieces of the buckle, and to come up under the mouth of the tortoise, hooking over the head of the beast in front. This strap must have been notched to fit over the head of the beast and therefore was adjustable. In order to accommodate the strap, there had to be a gap between the upper and lower sections of the buckle. However, as discussed earlier, it is virtually impossible to fabricate two layers of openwork design in piece-mold casting. This problem was solved by casting the upper and lower pieces of the buckle separately and soldering them together, an innovative technique at the time. There are slight overflows onto both parts of the buckle from the thin line of different colored material between them, positive evidence of soldering.

Although the quality of bronzes cast at some regional foundries during the Western Zhou dynasty and early Spring and Autumn period was not particularly high, the piece-mold technique had developed to the extent that it permitted relative freedom in the creation of forms and decorative schemes. Continued experimentation with this developed technology and the addition of new techniques such as lost-wax casting, and soldering and other methods of attachment, allowed for the expression of regional tastes in function, form, and decoration. Major trends in bronze decor and vessel types during the Western Zhou and the Spring and Autumn period included first a change to suit the tastes of the new Zhou rulers, and then an increase in regional styles as Zhou rule and centralized power collapsed. By the end of this period, changes in social, economic, and philosophical systems led to the beginnings of a market economy and attempts by new powers to re-unify China. This in turn led to exchanges of art both as booty and as market items, thus increasing influence among the various regional styles.

III: The Late Spring and Autumn Period to the Early Western Han Dynasty

By around 500 B.C. a relatively small number of dominant cultures had emerged in China and a trend toward unification had begun. This move was seen in economic developments, in political and military campaigns, and in philosophical and social change. The implications of a developing market economy with a monetary base to the spread of culture and artistic styles has been discussed earlier. Military and political campaigns took the form of larger or more powerful states annihilating their smaller or weaker neighbors and negotiating treaties with other states, forming hegemonies. The breakdown of the Zhou feudal system led to social and philosophical developments most dramatically illustrated by the large numbers of well-educated descendants of feudal lords who were unable to find employment in their native states due to their sheer numbers and by the inability of the system to absorb them. They roamed from state to state seeking an environment in which their talents, be they administrative, military, or philosophical, could be appreciated. Through their travels they facilitated the exchange of ideas and the developing consciousness of China as a whole. In 220 B.C., the Qin state from northwest China conquered the last opposing state and unified China. This unity was guaranteed in 206 B.C. with the emergence of the powerful Han dynasty.

Changes in preferred use and decoration of ritual vessels during this period presented a great challenge to those working in bronze. Also, around 500 B.C. the technology to produce iron had been developed in China, and bronze was beginning to lose its primacy. Other media, such as lacquer, a variety of ceramics, and painting on silk had begun to compete with bronze for objects intended for burial, ritual, or day-to-day use. Rapid and dramatic changes in philosophy affected the function of ritual vessels and led to a marked diminution of their use as well as a total change in their character. An interest in representation and pattern for its own sake marks the continuation of a trend toward secularization initiated at the beginning of the Western Zhou, and increasing numbers of bronzes were made as luxury items, with little or no ritual function or content.

One result of competition with other media was the development of new techniques that expanded the decorative potential of bronze. Lost-wax casting, which had first appeared somewhat earlier, was expanded, as was the practice of soldering and other methods of combining vessel parts. Vessels with new and even startling effects resulted from these advances.[27] The adaptation from foreign sources of the techniques for gilding and inlay made it possible to create painterly effects on the surface of bronzes and to create objects that directly competed with painted lacquers and ceramics.

A number of the issues that influenced the development of bronzes in the late Spring and Autumn and Warring States periods appear in the *ib* (no. 13). It is one of a group of thin-bodied bronze vessels with incised pictorial designs that have been dis-

26

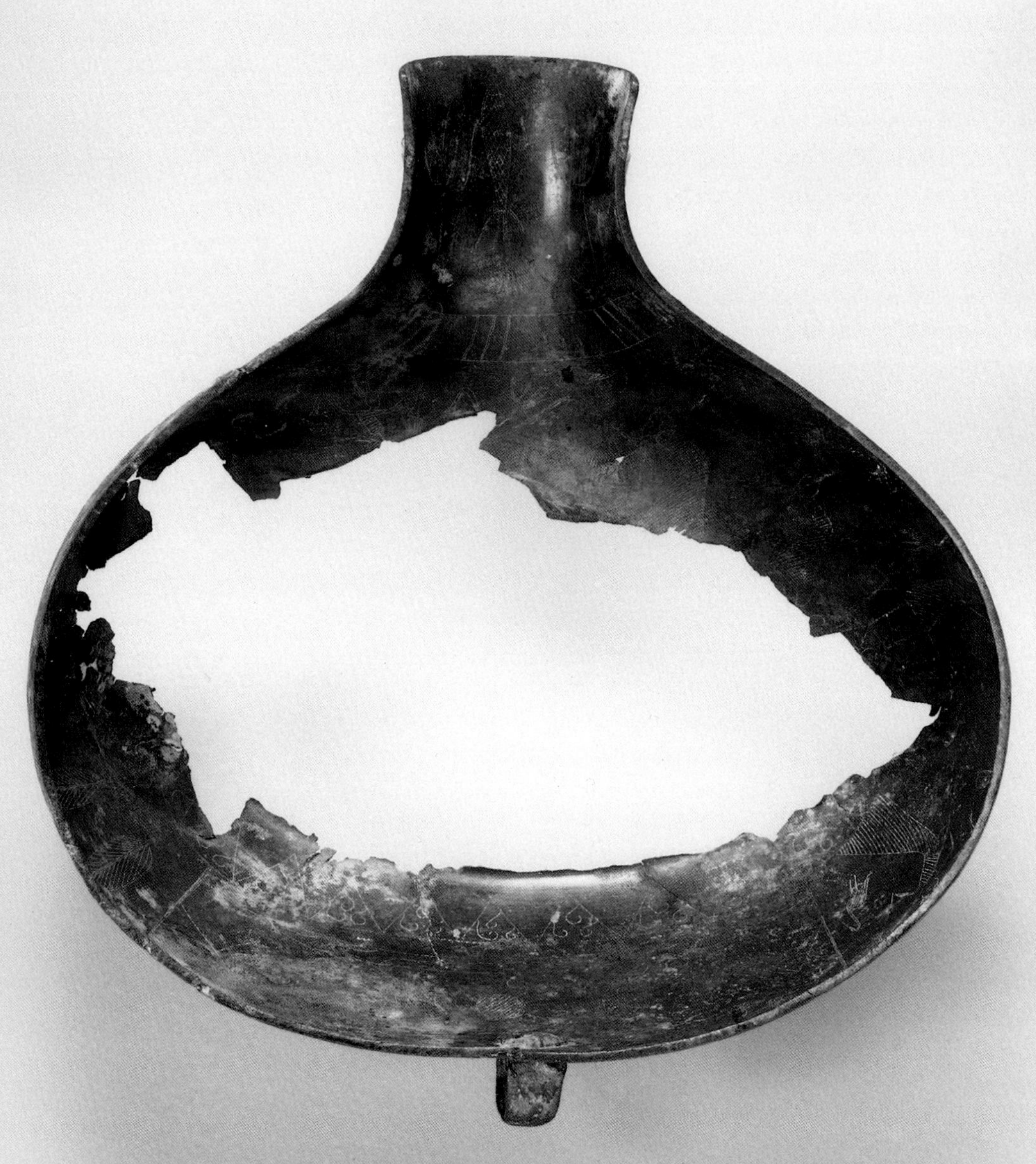

covered in sites over a broad geographical range. This vessel presents a number of interesting departures from earlier ritual bronzes. The remarkably thin body has every indication of being formed, rather than cast. The vessel is considerably thicker along the rim than it is in the well, suggesting that it was formed over a blank made of wood or some other material.[28] Although there is some evidence for forged objects from the very beginning of the Bronze Age, ritual vessels were cast from the early Shang until the appearance of this group at the end of the Spring and Autumn period. The handle on this vessel is mechanically attached to the body rather than cast on or soldered. The end of the handle penetrates a hole in the body and then is hammered flat, somewhat like riveting, to secure it to the vessel.

The outside of this *ib* is undecorated except for thin layers of red and black lacquer.[29] Although lacquer was used to highlight designs on vessels from perhaps as early as the Shang dynasty, the total reliance upon painted surface for the decorative effects on a large area of a bronze vessel is a new development in the late Spring and Autumn period. Perhaps the most interesting innovation on this group of vessels is the pictorial decoration and the technique used to create it. The designs are incised into the surface, indicating that a tool made of iron or some other material harder than bronze was used.

In recent years, improved excavation tech-

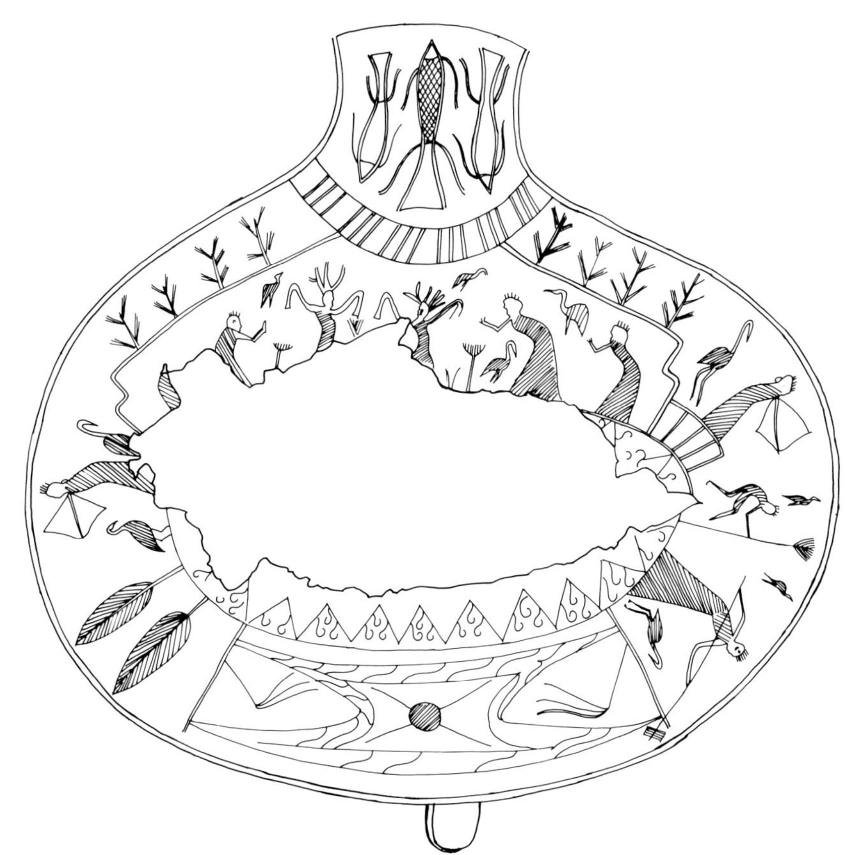

Opposite: No. 13. *Ib,* late Spring and Autumn period–early Warring States period, 6th–5th century B.C., 3″ x 8 ½,″ Eugene Fuller Memorial Collection, 51.43

Drawing showing the designs on the *ib* (no. 13).

niques have led to the discovery of more examples of what was once thought to be a very rare type. Because of their very thin bodies, these vessels are susceptible to breakage and corrosion; most examples that have been found are fragmentary. The consistent character of their shape and decoration suggests that these vessels were created at a single foundry; however, because of their widespread distribution, the foundry's location remains unclear. The earliest known examples of this type of vessel date from the late Spring and Autumn period (c. 500 B.C.). Decorative motifs on these vessels are of two types, abstract zoomorphs and figures. Those with figures often include settings such as buildings, trees, streams, and rocks and are among the earliest surviving examples of a developed pictorial art in China.[30] This *ih* with its pictorial decoration is an example of a type that dates to the end of the Spring and Autumn period.[31]

The design on this *ih* was made by using a narrow chisel or burin with repeated cuts one on top of the other, creating the appearance of a continuous line. Owing to corrosion and damage, some decoration and sections of the body have been lost. The decoration begins at the spout with three fish with long tendrils; the center fish faces the mouth, and the other two face the body of the vessel. A border of two widely spaced parallel lines connected by groups of perpendicular lines arranged in groups of three separates this segment from the rest of the bowl. Along the top of the vessel on either side of the spout are two groups of plants. They are depicted on a groundline that bends at the end of the plants and makes a second curve before it continues vertically to a point where it meets the base line in the center of the bowl. This groundline divides the interior of the *ih* into two scenes, one directly under the spout, the second continuing along the back of the vessel.

Beneath the spout are two dancing figures with elaborate headdresses and long-sleeved gowns. They face each other in a three-quarter back profile and, despite the obvious limitations of the technique, are depicted in some detail. Between the two figures is the end of a shaft with a crescent-shaped top filled with vertical lines; much of this shaft has been lost to damage. Behind each dancer is a second bent figure, each with spiky hair and short-sleeved gown. The figure to the left is reaching up and appears either to have released or is attempting to grab a small flying bird. The figure to the right also appears to have released a bird and is bent over another larger bird, obviously a crane. Between each of these two figures and the dancers is an upright shaft similar to the one between the dancers. Behind each of the bent figures is another engaged in a similar activity. The vertical lines descending from the groundline for the plants effectively serves as a frame behind this set of figures.

Continuing to the right of this framed area, near the top of the boundary, is a single large crane, then a figure standing on a four-legged platform. This figure, also with short hair and a short-sleeved gown, is drawing a bow. Next is a bent figure who appears to be planting in the ground a standard with a bushy, fan-shaped top; a pair of birds flies away from the top of this standard. A second figure holding a similar standard at a diagonal follows. In front of this figure is another large crane, then a long upright shaft. This shaft is connected to another similar shaft on the opposite side of the handle by a series of lines and other devices. In the center between the two shafts is a circle filled with diagonal lines, a target for the archer, the two shafts are supports for the target. Following the second support for the target is a pair of bushy trees and a crane, then another archer. This entire group is involved in an archery competition. The scene ends with a crane that faces the vertical line dividing it from the dance scene.

These two scenes are separated from the bottom of the bowl by a series of triangular devices that have evolved from the blade-shaped motifs on Shang bronzes. Each of the pendant triangles on this *ih* is decorated with three scrolling lines; the upright triangles are plain; these triangles are bordered above and below by a continuous line. The bottom of this vessel is completely lost and there is no trace of any decoration below the row of triangles.

This vessel and the general group to which it belongs pose some interesting questions concerning purpose, function, and iconography. The massive scale and number of bronze artifacts found in tombs of the same period, and even in the same tombs as these thin-bodied ones, indicate that there was no shortage of bronze, and economy of material does not seem to be the primary reason for creating them. Although forming the thin bodies over a previously designed blank might require less time and effort than piece-mold casting, cutting the designs into the surface must have been far more difficult than creating similar designs in clay, particularly with the use of stamps and other methods of producing molds that were common at the time. A partial explanation might be found in the freedom for direct expression that such a technique allowed.

The bodies of this group are so thin and fragile as to render them practically useless as vessels. The lacquer on the outside of this *ih* indicates that it could not have been heated or used to hold hot liquids, the expansion resulting from heating a thin bronze vessel would be much more dramatic than that of heating lacquer, thus the lacquer would tend to peel off. It is likely that the function of this group was largely ritual or ceremonial.

The scenes found on this group of vessels are somewhat different than those found on other types of pictorial bronzes of the same period, which tend to feature hunting, animal combat, or complex court rituals. The convention for the *ih* of this thin-bodied group is to begin with the spout decorated with three fish, and then two or more scenes that frequently incorporate plants, birds, and human figures. The birds do not appear to be the object of a hunt but rather play a part in ceremonies. The scene depicted at the front of this *ih* is a ritual dance with dancers in elaborate headdress and long-sleeved gowns attended by other figures. The relationship of this dance to the plants and the fish may indicate a fertility rite or seaonal sacrifice to guarantee good harvests. The rear scene on the *ih* is an archery competition. Such competitions were important in court ritual during the Zhou and were part of the training and discipline of the aristocracy.[32]

Although the decoration is limited by the technique, the range accomplished indicates a developing pictorial art. The figures are all arranged on a groundline; a primitive indication of a spatial relationship appears in the archers and the target; and the surface of the vessel is divided into a number of coherent scenes. A variety of representational effects are also accomplished. For example, the drapery on the figures is depicted with diagonal strokes, and the direction of these strokes is altered to show change in drapery designs. Details such as heads, ears, hands, hair styles, or headdresses are also well portrayed. Animals and figures are depicted in a number of poses including profile, three-quarter front profile, and three-quarter back profile. These poses often reveal a great deal of activity: dancers are caught in midstep with sleeves flying, archers with their bows fully drawn, birds in flight or marching along with one foot raised. Much of this detail shows

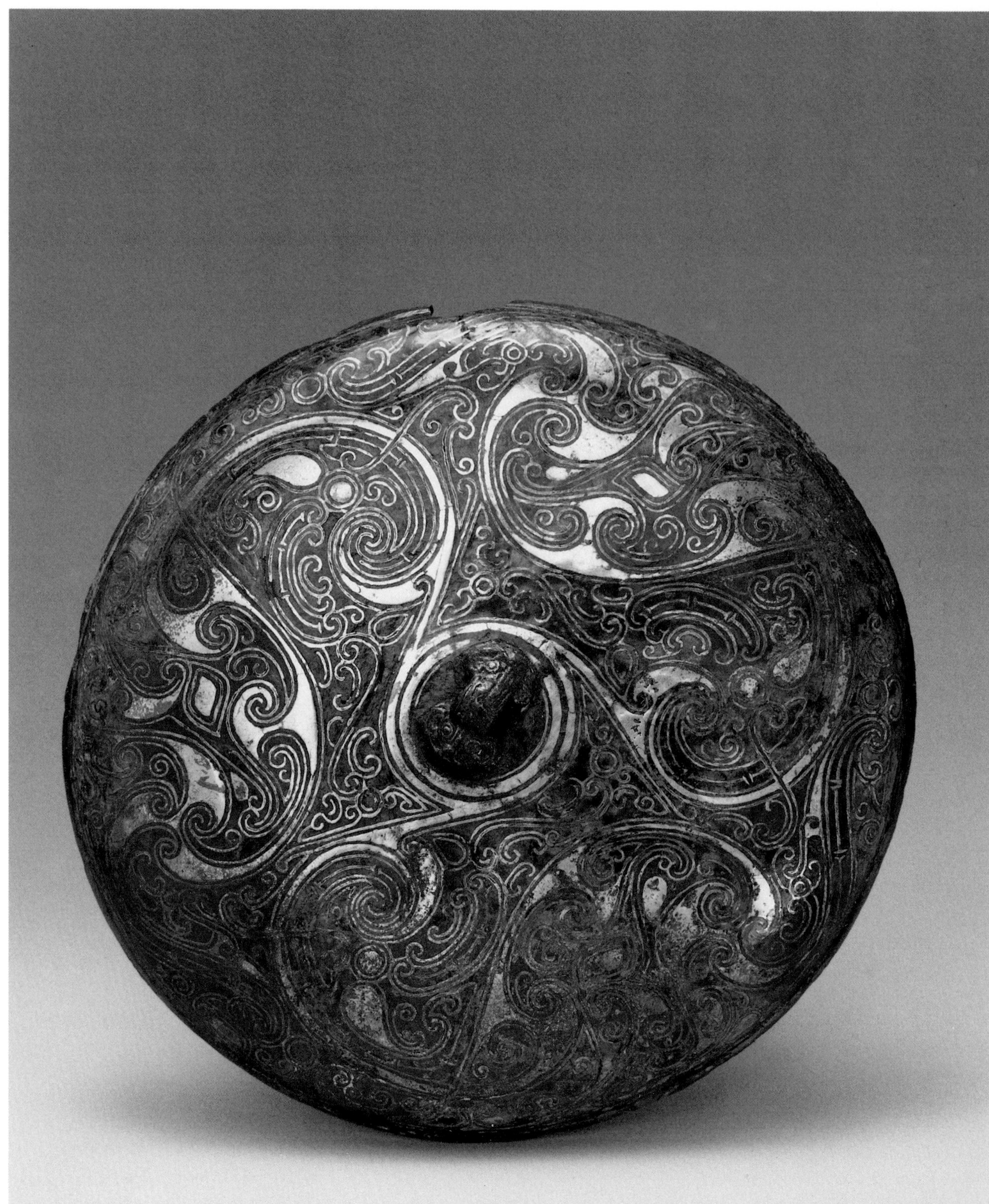

direct influence from the developing arts of painting, textiles, and lacquer.[33]

The lid (no. 14) is another example of a bronze vessel that displays influence from other media. Its silver inlay creates a series of flowing curvilinear patterns typical of lacquer and textile designs of the late fourth and early third century B.C.[34] Like the pictorial decoration on the *ih* (no. 13), these are two-dimensional in nature; they do not rely upon being raised above or cut below the surface of the vessel for their decorative effects as in the majority of earlier bronzes. The inlaid silver on this lid is flush with the surface of the bronze, and the designs, like the painted designs on lacquer and the woven, embroidered, or painted designs on textiles, are distinguished by contrasting bands of color.

Whereas the designs engraved on the *ih* required only a single although painstaking step, the application of the designs on this lid was technically complex. As with earlier bronzes, the designs first had to be created in the mold as slightly raised relief; they were then cast into the bronze, resulting in slightly depressed areas. Thin sheets of the inlay material were cut and hammered into the depressions. The inlay technique originated outside of China and early examples of this type reveal foreign sources. However, by the late Warring States period, when this lid was created, these techniques and motifs had been absorbed by the Chinese metalworking industry, and their decorative potential was applied to designs that relate to those on other media such as painted lacquer.[35]

The complex designs on this lid actually consist of one large unit repeated three times. Each unit flows from the central circle surrounding the handle. Broad bands of silver inlay spiral out from it in abstract patterns with many hooks and volutes to the outside edge. These designs are similar to patterns that appear on lacquers; as the so-called "cloud pattern," they make up much of the background design on bronzes and lacquers of the late Warring States period and the Western Han dynasty. The space between these broad areas of inlay are filled with finer lines that form tendrils which sometimes appear to cross over each other, or over the broader motifs. At certain points these tendrils take on almost zoomorphic shapes; a design that looks like a plumed bird with a small beak and large round eye occurs with some regularity.

A continuation into the Han dynasty of the emphasis on elegance and sumptuous decoration is seen in the gilt bronze bowl (no. 15). Gilding is a technique that arrived in China during the Warring States period and increased in popularity as its full decorative potential became understood. Like the lacquer on the *ih* (no. 13), gilding was applied onto the surface of an existing bronze. The process involved suspending finely ground gold in mercury and painting it on the vessel. When heated, the mercury vaporized and the gold melted and fused to the surface in a thin, uniform layer. Although this technique did not allow the freedom of paint or lacquer, it did provide the potential for covering entire vessels or sculptural forms with a uniform gold surface.[36]

Swirling cloud patterns cover almost all surfaces of this vessel. These patterns are closely related to the patterns on the inlaid lid (no. 14) and to patterns that also appear on painted lacquers as well as a number of other Han artifacts. On this vessel, these patterns are cut through the gilt into the bronze with a chisel or burin, in a technique very similar to that used in decorating the Warring States *ih* (no. 13). The technique is particularly effective in this case because the small chisel patterns reveal the bronze, creating a contrast in color as

Opposite: No. 14. Lid, late Warring States period, late 4th century B.C., 5/8" x 4 3/8," Eugene Fuller Memorial Collection, 36.11

No. 15. Bowl, Western Han dynasty, 206 B.C.–A.D. 24, 2 ⅛″ x 6 ¾,″ purchased in honor of Mrs. Coe V. Malone by her friends and the staff and trustees of the Seattle Art Museum with additional funds from the Margaret E. Fuller Purchase Fund on the occasion of her retirement on June 30, 1988, after 55 years on the staff, 88.25

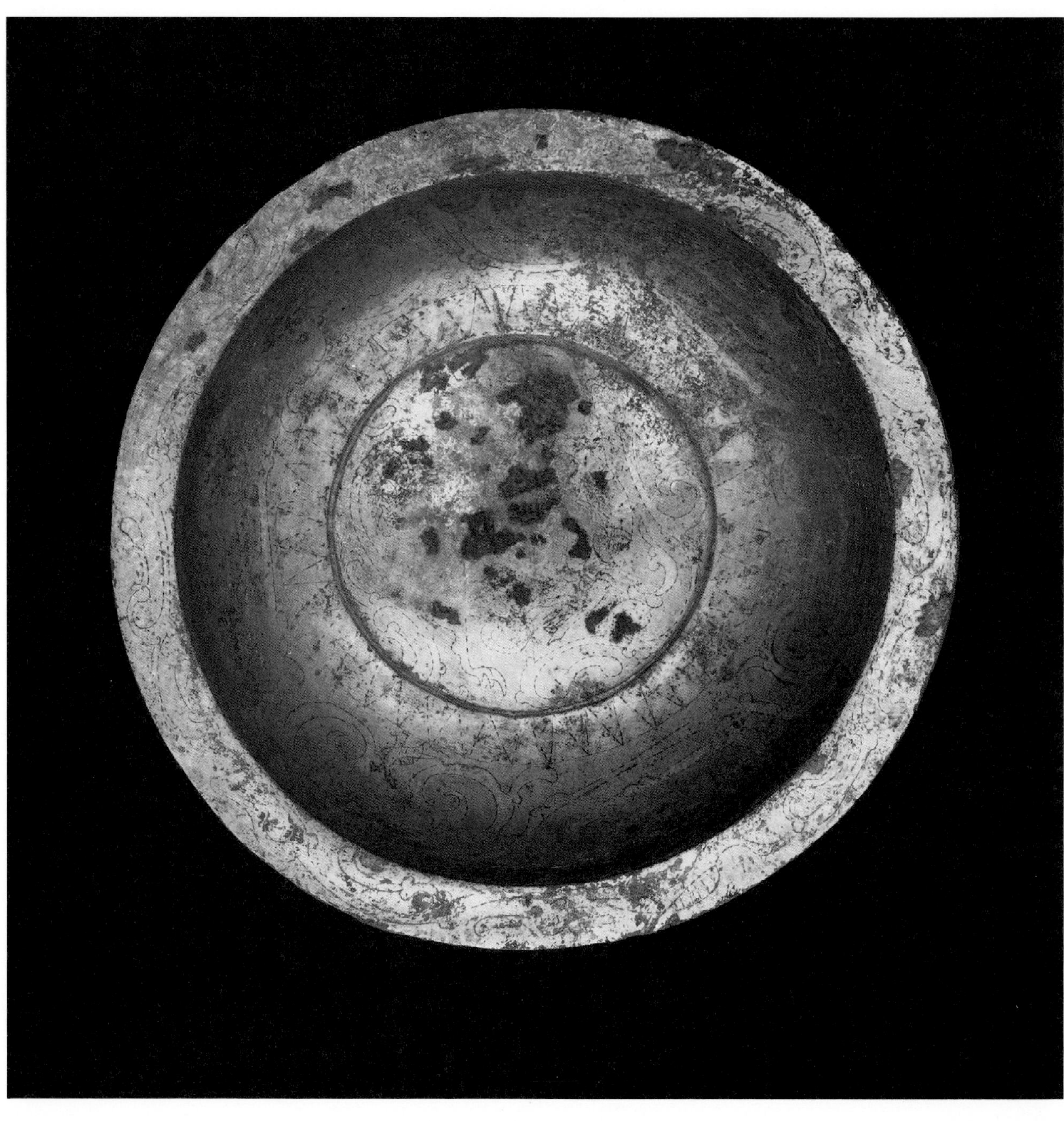

well as texture. Scattered through these cloud patterns are a number of small animals which further enliven the surface and provide examples of the developing iconography of the Western Han.

A deer is depicted on the bottom of the vessel inside the ring foot. Both of its front legs and one of its rear legs extend forward while the second rear leg is drawn back; the head looks back twisting the body. In the clouds in the first band of decor on the outside of the vessel is a small bird. A pair of similar birds appears on the rim of the vessel and again near the top of the decoration inside. Between the pair of birds inside is a marvelous rabbit; two more birds appear lower down. Typical of Western Han decoration, these animals are arranged in rows that face in opposing directions: the birds on the rim and inside near the base face in a counterclockwise direction, while those inside near the top face clockwise. The designs in the well are slightly corroded and difficult to read. The top and bottom of the inside of the vessel are bordered by rows of upright triangles related to those seen in the earlier *ih* and also to the patterns seen on Western Han bronze mirrors.[37]

The gilt bronze bowl marks the end of a long development that began with the earliest of the Shang ritual vessels. The first step in this development was a technology allowing the creation in bronze of vessels based on Neolithic period ceramic prototypes. As mastery of this technology increased, vessel shape and decoration evolved away from ceramic prototypes to a fuller exploitation of the plastic potential of bronze. New shapes and types of implements that were unique to bronze also appeared. By the beginning of the Western Zhou, the technology had evolved to a sufficient level to meet the new challenges created by changes in ritual systems and the function and decoration of the implements used in them. Late in the Spring and Autumn and the Warring States periods the appearance of iron, which was superior to bronze for tools and weapons, as well as changes in ritual and philosophy and increased interest in the two-dimensional decoration of painting, lacquers, and textiles, resulted in a final burst of creative energy and innovation in the medium of bronze. New techniques introduced at this time continued to influence bronze technology long after the casting of ritual implements had ceased to be its primary application.

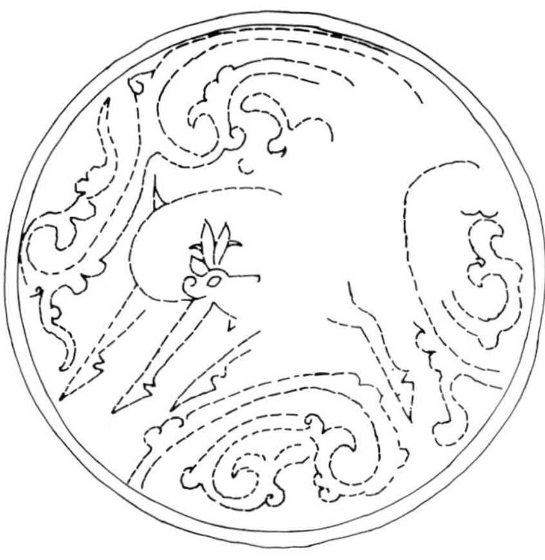

Drawing illustrating the main design in the center of the underside of the bowl (no. 15).

Notes

1. A second possible technique is that the interior core was first created, then hardened, and a set of clay slabs the desired thickness of the walls of the piece placed on it. The initial carving of designs was done in the positive on these slabs. A second set of clay slabs was applied over these to take the design in the negative and create the mold. After disassemby, the first set of slabs was disposed of, then the process was similar to that discussed above. However, no evidence of slabs with designs in the positive are known to this author.

2. The exceptions are low, flat vessels such as the *pan,* which may be decorated on the inside, outside, or both.

3. The relationship between the development of ritual and implement is difficult to define. Certainly ritual function did influence the shape and decoration of many vessels. However, certain catagories of ritual implements, such as bells, have limited pre-Bronze Age prototypes and the rituals they were used in could only have evolved after, or hand in hand, with their development.

4. Hayashi Minao has speculated on the iconography of the *taotie* based on the study of later texts and usage. *Shang and Zhou Bronzes,* II, pp. 20-90. Contemporary writings give no information on the significance of this creature. It has been suggested that the *taotie* is in part a solution to the problem of portraying a three-dimensional animal on a two-dimensional surface. David Keightley provides an imaginative setting for the use of Shang vessels and makes extensive use of the oracle bone libraries to document Shang history and ritual practices. *Sources of Shang History,* pp. 1-2. In none of these inscriptions or in the many others that have been translated or transcribed does the term *taotie* appear. The use of the bovine and rams for sacrifice is frequently mentioned and may explain the popularity of these motifs on ritual bronzes of the Anyang period.

5. See Weng Fong, ed., *The Great Bronze Age of China,* pp. 75-76 for a discussion of early bronze *jue* and evidence of forging and other methods of metalworking.

6. In Wen Fong, ed., *The Great Bronze Age of China* pieces of this style are dated to the Zhengzhou phase of the Shang dynasty (roughly 16th-14th century B.C.). See for instance no. 9, p. 107 which comes from the Shang sites at Panlongcheng in Hubei province. Hayashi Minao dates the Seattle piece to phase I of the Middle Yin period. *Shang and Zhou Bronzes, Illustrations,* I, p. 164, pl. 11.

7. Hayashi Minao dates this piece to his Late Yin phase II, type 2. *Shang and Zhou Bronzes,* I, p. 166, pl. 45.

8. The flange has long been discussed as a device developed to hide the marks created by the different sections of the mold. Certainly the two flanges under the spout on this *jue* may have served that purpose. However, the flange also appears to have been used compositionally to add balance, to delineate areas of design, or to separate elements of a motif such as the two halves of a *taotie.*

9. See Hayashi, *Shang and Zhou Bronzes, Illustrations,* I, p. 166, pl. 45. This same inscription appears on a *ding* and a series of *nao* bells he dates Late Yin phase II, *Shang and Zhou Bronzes,* I, p. 7, pl. 5.

10. See Hayashi, *Shang and Zhou Bronzes, Illustrations,* I, p. 178, pl. 45.

11. A number of recognizable animals such as the ram and the bovine appear on vessels of the late Anyang period. The reason for the addition of these animals to the existing vocabulary of composite creatures remains open to speculation. Certainly the bovine and the ram played an important role in the ritual sacrifices described in the oracle bones of the late Anyang period.

12. The phoenix in Shang rituals is discussed in Hayashi, *Shang and Zhou Bronzes,* II, pp. 132-46.

13. The upper element might be read as a trunk, the middle element a tusk, and the lower the jaw of an elephantlike creature. The eye, plume, thin body, curled tail, and two small legs are similar to other composite creatures of the Shang. The elephant is not unknown on Shang dynasty bronzes, but usually is more easily recognized as an elephant than in this case.

14. The *taotie* and other forms of dragons are discussed in Hayashi, *Shang and Zhou Bronzes,* II, pp. 20-132.

15. The bird-biting beast is discussed in Hayashi, *Shang and Zhou Bronzes,* II, pp. 37-40.

16. Hayashi Minao illustrates a Late Yin phase II *ding* with the same inscription in *Shang and Zhou Bronzes, Illustrations,* I, p. 6, pl. 73. The design on the Seattle piece, however, is closer to the *ding* in St. Louis, ibid., p. 9, pl. 96. The inscription is one of a group, *Shang and Zhou Bronzes,* I, pp. 15-16, type 19.

17. Hayashi Minao suggests that this device, which he defines as a spatula-shaped pair of horns, is an indication of status. *Shang and Zhou Bronzes,* II, pp. 17-19.

18. Hayashi Minao has identified these creatures as bird/dragons. *Shang and Zhou Bronzes,* II, pp. 127-31.

19. Hayashi Minao dates this vessel to the late phase of the Anyang period of the Shang dynasty, roughly contemporary with the round *ding* and much later than the earlier use of this type of decoration. *Shang and Zhou Bronzes, Illustrations,* I, p. 38, pl. 21.

20. The handles on this vessel begin at the very base with a gape-jawed animal with large teeth and small ears that bites the handle. These are followed by bovine or ram heads with extravagantly curled horns, large eyes, and striated eyebrows. The rest of the handle is relatively simple, with scales on the edges and three spade-shaped designs on the outside. The inside of the handle is hollow and largely covered with soil. A stub or sprue is visible in the top and bottom of the inside of each handle. It has been suggested that these handles are modern additions, and certainly they have been cast onto the vessel in an untidy manner. Overflows cover parts of the dragon and *leiwen* in the upper band and the leg of one of the pendant dragons in the middle band. The animal on the handle is not uncommon, but the horns are unusually exuberant, and their scale is somewhat out of proportion with the rest of the vessel. However, the patina is consis-

tent with the rest of the vessel and penetrates deeply into the bronze, a fair indication of age. The decor on the handle is consistent with that on other Shang vessels and with that on the vessel itself. It seems more likely that these handles were cast on shortly after the vessel was created to replace a failed cast or breakage. This would explain the overflows and the stumps that appear on the bottom of the inside of the handle.

21. A similar piece in the Arthur M. Sackler Collection at the Smithsonian Institution is reproduced in Hayashi, *Shang and Zhou Bronzes, Illustrations,* I, p. 109, pl. 24, and is dated Western Zhou phase II, style 6.

22. Hayashi Minao places the earliest examples of the type of design in Late Yin phase I, type 1. *Shang and Zhou Bronzes, Illustrations,* I, p. 2, pl. 15

23. A *gui* provides a precise cyclical date for the Zhou overthrow of the Shang. Unfortunately, without a point of reference, it is impossible to place this date precisely. It has been suggested that it corresponds to 1052 B.C. Wen Fong, ed., *The Great Bronze Age of China,* p. 203, no. 41.

24. Although the significance of the *taotie* and other designs on the surface of the bronzes of the Shang dynasty is not entirely clear, the frequency of their appearance suggests they had some importance. The relatively rapid evolution of these designs into abstract patterns during the Western Zhou suggest they did not have an equal importance to the Zhou people. Hayashi Minao has attempted to trace the meaning of these motifs back from Han examples which are identified by characters in Han texts. *Shang and Zhou Bronzes,* II, pp. 18-20. Whether the iconography of the Han is the same as that of the Shang and Zhou is difficult to determine.

25. White, *Tombs of Old Lo-yang,* p. 165, no. 513, pl. CLXXVI.

26. The issues of transport of materials during this period, be it copper or bronze in ingots, or finished vessels, remain unresolved. Certainly some refinement was done near the mining site and it seems that the copper found at Tonglushan was transported as ingots.

27. The earliest known surviving example of the use of lost-wax casting in China is the altar platform from the tomb of the Prince of the Kingdom of Chu found at Xiasi, Xichuan, Henan province. This tomb dates to the sixth century B.C. Ren Changzhong and Wang Changqing, "The Casting and Restoration of the Bronze Altar Table," pp. 474-78. Innovative examples of the use of lost-wax casting and soldering can be seen in some of the vessels found at the tomb of the Marquis Yi of the State of Zeng at Suixian, Hubei province, dating to around 433 B.C.

28. No studies of the method used to fashion this type of vessel or of the type of metal used have been carried out. The consistency of shapes, including the flat *pan* and the *ih,* indicate that some type of blank was used and the metal was worked around it by hammering and bending. The method of creating the vessel and of applying the designs suggests a fairly soft and malleable material, perhaps a bronze alloy with a high copper content. Charles D. Weber comes to a similar conclusion. "Chinese Pictorial Bronzes," p. 271.

29. The use of lacquer on bronze is rare but not unknown. Certain vessels from the Shang dynasty are thought to be coated with lacquer and some vessels of the Zhou have designs highlighted by applications of black lacquer. Personal conversation, Tadanori Yuba, Idemitsu Museum of Arts. A covered *jun* with gold and silver inlay excavated from a late 4th-century B.C. tomb at Baoshan, Jingmen, Hubei province, has the remains of a thick coat of lacquer on the interior. Much of it has lifted or has been lost. Bronze mirrors dating from the Warring States period have been found with lacquer decoration on the back; an example is a small square mirror from Yutaishan, Jingzhou, Hubei province.

30. Pictorial bronzes of this type are discussed by Charles D. Weber, in "Chinese Pictorial Bronzes," pp. 271-312, and by Yie Xiaoyan, "Engraved Bronzes," pp. 158-64. For other examples see The Zhenjiang Museum, "The Eastern Zhou Tomb at Wangjiasahn," pp. 24-37. See also Salmony, *Antler and Tongue,* pp. 14-15.

31. See the *ih* and *pan* with very similar designs excavated from the Late Spring and Autumn period tomb at Changsha. The Hunan Provincial Museum, "The Chu Tombs of Changsha," p. 49.

32. For a discussion of archery as a ceremony in the Western Zhou dynasty see Lie Yu, "Archery as a Ceremony," pp. 1112-20.

33. There are several extant examples of the effect artists in the southern state of Chu were able to accomplish with painting. For examples, see Li Xueqin, *Eastern Zhou and Qin Civilizations,* pp. 435-46.

34. For a discussion of the arts of lacquers and textiles from this period see Li Xuiqin, *Eastern Zhou and Qin Civilizations,"* pp. 342-70.

35. See Jenny F. So, "New Departures in Eastern Zhou Bronze Designs," in *The Great Bronze Age of China,* Wen Fong, ed. pp. 261-62, and "The Inlaid Bronzes of the Warring States Period," for discussions of the origin and development of inlaid bronzes during the Spring and Autumn period and the Warring States period, ibid., pp. 305-308. This lid is of So's Type III and reveals influence from the southern art of painted lacquer in its abstract curvilinear motifs. A nearly identical lid has been excavated from a late 4th-century B.C. tomb at Baoshan, Jingmen, Hubei province. Lids of similar style have also been found in tombs 246 and 480 at Yutaishan, Jingzhou, Hubei province, suggesting that such lids were made in the late 4th century B.C. for the Kingdom of Chu and were influenced by the highly developed lacquer arts of that kingdom. See Hayashi Minao, *Shang and Zhou Bronzes,* III, p. 216.

36. See Wen Fong, ed., *The Great Bronze Age of China,* p. 328.

37. For a discussion of these triangular-shaped devices in Western Han mirrors and Han dynasty iconography, see Loewe, *Ways to Paradise,* pp. 66-85.

Bibliography

The Baoshan Cemetery Systemization Group of the Jingsha Railroad Archaeological Team, "Excavation of the Chu Tomb at Baoshan in the City of Jingmen," *Wenwu,* 1988.5, pp. 1-15.

Hayashi Minao. *A Conspectus of Shang and Zhou Bronzes,* 3 vols. Yoshikawa Kōbunkan, Tokyo, 1984-88.

The Hunan Provincial Museum. "The Chu Tombs of Changsha," *Kaogu Xuebao,* 1959.1, p. 49.

Keightley, David. *Sources of Shang History: The Oracle-bone Inscriptions of Bronze Age China.* Berkeley: University of California Press, 1978.

Li Hsiao-ting. *Chia-ku-wen-tzu Chi shih.* Taipei: Institute of History and Philology, 1965.

Li Xueqin. *Eastern Zhou and Qin Civilizations.* Trans. by K. C. Chang. New Haven: Yale University Press, 1985.

Liu Yu. "Archery as a Ceremony Reflected in the Bronze Inscriptions of the Western Zhou Dynasty," *Kaogu,* 1986.12, pp. 1112-20.

Loewe, Michael. *Ways to Paradise: The Chinese Quest for Immortality.* London: George Allen & Unwin, 1979.

Ren Changzhong and Wang Changqing. "The Casting and Restoration of the Bronze Altar Table with Cloud Patterns of the Spring and Autumn Period from Xiasi, Xichuan, Henan," *Kaogu,* 1987.5, pp. 474-78.

Salmony, Alfred. *Antler and Tongue: An Essay on Ancient Chinese Symbolism.* Ascona: Artibus Asiae, 1954.

Weber, Charles D. "Chinese Pictorial Bronzes of the Late Chou Period, Part II, Group IV: Vessels with Scenes in Engraved Line," *Artibus Asiae,* 28, 1966, pp. 271-312.

Wen Fong, ed. *The Great Bronze Age of China.* New York: The Metropolitan Museum of Art, 1981.

White, William Charles. *Tombs of Old Lo-yang.* Shanghai: Kelly and Walsh, 1934.

Yie Xiaoyan. "Engraved Bronzes of the Eastern Zhou Dynasty," *Kaogu,* 1983.2, pp. 158-164.

The Zhenjiang Museum. "The Eastern Zhou Tomb at Wangjiashan in Jianbi, Zhenjiang, Jiangsu," *Wenwu,* 1987.12, pp. 24-37.